A Man on Many Missions

A Man on Many Missions

Adam C. Mattocks

&

Derk R. Mattocks (Co-Author)

CITIOFBOOKS, INC.
3736 Eubank NE Suite A1
Albuquerque, NM 87111-3579
www.citiofbooks.com
Hotline: 1 (877) 389-2759
Fax: 1 (505) 930-7244

Ordering Information:
Quantity sales. Special discounts are available on quantity purchases by corporations, associations, and others. For details, contact the publisher at the address above.

Printed in the United States of America.

ISBN-13:		
	Paperback	978-1-963209-33-4
	eBook	978-1-963209-35-8
	Hardcover	978-1-963209-34-1

Library of Congress Control Number: 2024900477

Table Of Contents

Dedication 1

Acknowledgment 3

About the Author... 5

Chapter 1 7

Chapter 2 12

Chapter 3 18

Chapter 4 26

Chapter 5 47

Chapter 6 59

Chapter 7 69

Dedication

I dedicate this to The LORD my God, whose foreknowledge and provisions provided me with everybody and anything I needed at the right time in the right place while on my life journey.

Thank you, Lord, for my wife, formally *Annie Washington*, the love of my life. She has been my rock and constant companion.

My children *Barbara (Kaye), Katrina, Adam Christopher, Karen, Katia, and Adam Charles* are all who have grown up, traveling their respective journeys and writing their own stories. Stories anchored in their own family life, careers, and community service that would make any parent proud.

I am humbled that my grandsons *Shadrian Gayles and Benjamin Mattocks* both followed my path by joining the Air Force as I did, while another grandson, *Zachary Mattock*s, elected to go Marine Corps. All stood up and stood out to serve our country through military services. Also, like me, my granddaughter *Ahlivia Mattocks* completed pre-med biology with a focus on advancing medicine. All of us are carrying on a legacy to behold.

Lord, Thank you to my parents, *Ira "Poppa" Mattocks and Lilly (Frazzell) Mattocks,* and my brothers, *Ira Webster, Hubert Odell, Colon Frazzell, William Clen, and Ernest Nash. Sisters Ida B, Willie B (Lil Honey),* and T*helma Olivia.* Special siblings *Carrie Delaney* and *Jerry Mattocks.*

Extraordinary friends and family *Rowland Ellis, Derk "Mickey" Mattocks, Eulus Grant King, James Taylor, John Moses Monk,* and *Pearl Owens Monk.*

And so many others that were and are a godly blessing that it has become too many to name.

Acknowledgment

I thank the Lord for sending *Anne Washington* and allowing me to find that amazingly virtuous and ever-capable wife inside her. I trusted her from the beginning, and she greatly enriched my life. She gets up early to prepare breakfast for me and for her household, even when she had been up late into the night before. A hard and smart worker, she was always energetic, strong, and focused.

The Lord graced her with business insight and dealings, resulting in sustained profits and growth because of her great generosity in extending a helping hand to the poor and open arms to the needy. She was well known and respected by magistrates and city officials, civil and religious leaders, physicians and educators, business owners, and entrepreneurs. She spoke truth to power and gave instructions seasoned with wisdom to the humble.

Thank you for allowing the former Ms. Anne Washington to become my wife, whom I adored and publicly praised for all.

Moreover, I would like to thank *Derk Mattocks' (Mickey) for his* outstanding contributions as a co-author of this book.

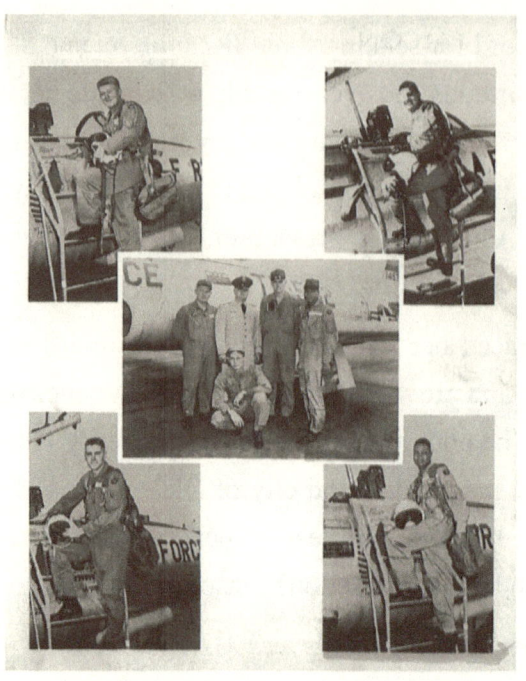

About the Author

Adam C. Mattocks' memoirs "A Man on Many Missions" speaks volumes to his commitment to helping others. His many achievements, and there were many, were doing for others, included but were not limited to:

Air Force Veteran: Serving his country in the United States Air force as a pilot from 1957 to 1964, where he specialized in flying aircraft such as the Lockheed T-33 Shooting Star Jet-Powered Trainer Aircraft, F-86, a transonic jet fighter aircraft, and the Boeing B-52 Strat fortress long-range, subsonic, jet-powered strategic bomber.

Following his military career, Mr. Mattocks' legacy supports that of a trailblazer breaking down berries and making pathways for others, as in:

Dees, Matt. Jacksonville Daily News: "*A Man on Many Missions, From B-52s to civil rights, Adam Mattocks has met the call to serve.*"

The Crash: This mission and its aftermath are captured in Adam Mattocks' book, "A Man on Many Missions," and the book The Goldsboro Broken Arrow.

The Fight for Black Pilots: Following his serving in the U.S. Air Force, Mr. Mattocks applied for but was denied each pilot position he sought with commercial airlines due to racial discrimination. He had little to no legal recourse unless he could clearly prove that racial discrimination was the reason he was not hired.

First Black Department Head: As Director of the Onslow County Fund for the underprivileged and War on Poverty.

Started Head: in Onslow County.

Implemented the Community Action Program: in various neighborhoods, which set up community centers to improve neighborhoods by conducting revitalization efforts and social justice programs.

Economic Improvement Board: He was a member of the Economic Improvement Board, which worked with County officials in establishing the Albert J. Ellis airport.

Chapter 1

Belonging to a segregated, underprivileged, rural, but blessed community, I did not have much growing up. Resources were scarce; hence I only wore one pair of shoes every day until they lost the resemblance to a shoe. I put cardboard inside the inner sole of my shoes to cover the holes to protect my feet from sand, gravel, and mud as I walked to and from school, among other places. Often, one of my shoes would break from the top, forcing me to walk in the mud barefoot. My mother had to stitch it together with string and sometimes, fine wire.

As I grew up with the kids in my community, we began making our own toys with the paltry resources at our disposal. From a cloth hanger, we made a rod that could be guided by a stick with a prong at its edge. Old, worn-out automobile tires were often on the radar for us to roll around and play with; we'd tie a rope to the tires, attach the rope to a tree limb and make swings. We had a lot of fun spanking and rolling old car tires, hoops, and metal hubs down narrow dirt roads and paths and around houses that did not have much grass to speak of.

Climbing trees was our favorite pastime. Many of us would climb on the same tree and place our weights on the limb, bending it to the ground and then get off together. The limb would spring back to its original position.

At times, when our boredom got the better of us, it forced us to be more creative and daring with our creations. We would make cars, trucks, and other sorts of vehicles with wooden wheels, hoods, and fenders with cutouts for windows and doors. We weren't the only builders in our community; my father and brothers built our family house in their free time. So, building stuff was in our blood.

In the 1960s, there was no electricity or running water in our community. Water came from wells or the ground. Dirt roads were rare as well; only cart paths were constructed.

The winters were perhaps the toughest of the year due to the lack of heating resources. My mother cooked with an old iron stove and heated the house with the available wood. We, the kids, would gather around the kerosene lamp to complete our homework. My mother would boil water so we could mix it with some cold water to take a bath, or the water would be too cold even to wash our hands.

Sundays were the best. My mother would prepare a big breakfast, and my father would have all of us sit down and thank God for his blessings. One of us would recite the scripture and pray for God's blessings. Then off to the Church we'd go. In quarterly meetings, each family would bring food to share with the others. This was an integral part of our community's tradition, and traditions like these helped build a strong bond within the community.

I was seven years of age when I was finally enrolled in a school, while not prestigious by any means, this school radiated love. It had a mere three rooms that housed all the students who attended. All the students from this underprivileged, but blessed community walked a three-mile distance to school. Only two black teachers taught all the classes from grades one through seven. The class arrangement consisted of four rows of seven seats, with me seated near the middle.

In my first and second grades, I could barely read. So, when the teachers gave the book to the first student to read, I would memorize the words and repeat them as if I was reading them. My tactics were discovered in third grade, and my parents were informed. My father was very concerned, and he went to the Board of Education and purchased a used third-grade reader.

My mother taught me three to five different words each night until I was able to read and spell them. My newly developed skill made me enjoy school, and I began having little problems with homework as well.

I attended Georgetown High School from fourth through 12th grade. During my time there, I studied Grammar and Mathematics. Despite this, my dream of flying never left me. I often sat on my porch before and after school, watching airplanes fly overhead. I told my teacher that I wanted to make an airplane as my school project, and both my father and teacher agreed. My mother even ordered a kit for me to build a 24-inch long, 36-inch wing-span model airplane. I followed the instructions, but unfortunately, the plane did not fly, even though it looked like the picture. However, the rubber band that powered the propeller did manage to pull the plane about 6-7 feet.

I have had a strong desire to fly an airplane since I was seven. As I grew older, my father continued his work as a tenant farmer and used his building trade skills for carpentry and masonry work. When his construction work became too demanding, my older brother and I took on more responsibilities on the farm. I became the leader on the farm, and together with my sisters, we broke ground for planting and tended to the crops using just four mules. Feeding, watering, and securing the stock each day was also our responsibility.

Eventually, we began using a large tractor to prepare the land for spring planting while the mules were used for lighter tasks. Later, my father acquired a plow pulled by two mules that could create rows for planting and cultivating crops. As my family, including my mother, sisters, and brother, worked on the farm, my older brothers contributed to the family's income through construction work, and our circumstances improved.

When I reached high school, my father purchased a one-row tractor. With this tractor, I could do all of the groundbreaking tilting the soil done previously by mules, but much faster. As a result, I had little time for extracurricular activities. Through hard work, our 100 plus acre farm was eventually paid off, and upon graduating from Georgetown high school in 1953, my father gifted me a 1953 Chevrolet Bel Air two-door hardtop car.

"This car is for you and your mother," said my father, handing me the keys to my new ride.

My mother, however, did not drive; hence I was to take her everywhere she needed to go. But she usually only went to Church since my family was very religious. I'd often accompany her on her visit and pay my appreciation to God for all he had blessed us with. God made our farm prosperous and replaced the holes in my shoes with soles. He also replaced our pants and patches with new pants. A house where you could tally the chickens through the floor and count the stars through the roof became a house that did not leak, and the wind that once entered through the cracks and windows now became a bad memory.

Despite all we had overcome, I wanted to do more. So, in the summer of 1953, I volunteered to enter each of the three service branches. I wished to return some of the favor to my family. Even though I was accepted to all services, none of them called me for active duty, but my classmates got called, even though they didn't even volunteer.

Having heard no response, in the fall of 1953, I placed an application to Agriculture and Technical College of North College at Greensboro, North Carolina, known today as North Carolina A&T State University. There, I majored in Biology with minors in Chemistry and Air Science.

It was a very hard struggle carrying twelve hours every quarter. This required a classroom and lab setting of twelve through fourteen hours each day. That September, I was ordered to report to Lackland Air Base in San Antonia, Texas, for evaluations and further assignments.

My first assignment to an Air Base was at Tyndale AFB, Florida. I met my first challenge as a black Air Force Cadet entering the Advance AFROTC from A&T University. Some of the white students would say openly and boldly that the Air Force would not have "niggers" flying its airplanes or that "niggers" aren't capable or qualified to fly the F84 and F86 airplanes.

"You'll see," was my response every time.

The hatred I was subject to during my time at Tyndale AFB, Florida, lit the fire inside me to succeed. I worked even harder as a junior and senior at A&T to graduate and be commissioned in four years. Like in high school, I didn't have much time for extracurricular activities like Pledging for fraternities. When I arrived back in my junior year, I was assigned to the flight unit that was made up of all students who did not desire to be part of the ROTC. They had not planned to volunteer for the Advance ROTC, and the only control you had was to issue demerits.

The cadets during the first two drill sessions on the field lacked enthusiasm but were still respectful. In the third session, I explained to them that I realized they did not wish to be there, so it was a waste of both their time and mine. I further informed them that I would not issue any demerits during the 1st and 2nd school quarters. However, I expected them to shape up by the third quarter and stand tall executing exact maneuvers to win the AF competition, and I wanted them to take the overall competition from the Army ROTC.

What happened at the first drills session of the third quarter amazed me. The AFROTC cadets moved with amazing accuracy and perfection. The cadets performed superbly during that week and were noted as number one in the Air Force ROTC competition and the Army and Air Force competitions, as well. Although these cadets' performance was the best overall, it was decided by the higher authority to give the award to the Army ROTC unit because we did not work to meet the standard throughout the school year and were not up to standard during the first two quarters.

Even though the award was denied, each cadet left this experience knowing that he had accomplished his assigned task with impressive precision. They made me and those in charge very proud. Some of those cadets who were not interested in ROTC continued on and got their commissions. I learned from this experience that leadership when used wisely, might be all you need to accomplish a mission.

Chapter 2

With determination and a strong sense of self-discipline, I persevered to achieve my goal of graduating in just four years. During each summer break, I returned home to lend a hand on the farm, where I helped harvest tobacco, corn, and beans. In 1957, I proudly received my Bachelor of Science degree in pre-med and biology, along with a commission as a 2nd Lieutenant in the U.S. Air Force. I was then sent to Lackland Air Force Base in Texas, where I underwent evaluation and orientation, along with some training. The final evaluation determined our future assignments in the Air Force, whether we were to be pilots or if we would work in another field.

My journey was marked by a mixture of confidence and humility. After graduating near the top of my high school class, I initially felt quite proud of myself. But when I arrived at A&T and saw the talent and achievements of my fellow classmates, I was humbled. Despite this setback, my experiences at A&T boosted my ego once more. But again, as I spent time at Lackland Air Force Base, I was quickly brought back down to earth; I was surrounded by many other talented 2nd Lieutenants from various universities and Air Force Academies across the United States.

All my academic experiences taught me that as my competition broadened, so did the challenges and with that came further struggle to stay among the best. During my competition with other Air Force officers to become a pilot, I quickly realized the disadvantages faced by black students who were educated in segregated schools in testing situations. Students at segregated white schools received the newest books and materials, from which the test was developed, and was based on advanced contemporary information. While those at segregated black schools received outdated and used books; to keep the kids handicapped. Despite these challenges, I remained steadfast in my determination to succeed.

It is disheartening to see that students from a school system relying on secondhand books and discarded materials do not perform as well on tests as those who have access to new books and materials. Although their intelligence is equal, the difference in the knowledge of "new" information present in the new books and missing from the older materials affects their test scores. This disparity in resources highlights the importance of ensuring that all students have equal access to quality education materials.

Despite the discriminatory attitude of segregated schools, there were prominent all black universities that did a marvelous job in educating the black children. During 50s and 60s, any black or white children could acquire advanced, and current information in prominent black universities without any segregation. Despite all the odds, the black teachers and administration had benefitted children considerably. I myself is the product of a black institution and feel immense proud in representing my alma meter.

Moving forward, I remember the enchanted moment when I was selected by the Air Force to enter flight training from a vast number of officers. There were approximately two hundreds officers; some brilliant ones. But, in an astounding stroke of luck, I was selected for the flight training after strict evaluation and training process. I fortunately received the orders to arrive at Spence Air Force Base, Moultrie, Georgia. Though, the worrying phase didn't end here.

At that time, the racism issue was at its peak in the America, which was quite stressful for me. This issue had me worrying and perturbing with the fear of settling in with the massive batch of white cadets and officers. In my head, I had already pictured Spence as a place of racism and Jim crow. But little did I know that the place would have my heart because of my fellows. Despite being the only black officer, I was welcomed with open arms and received pre-stated respect, sincerity, and warmth. Luckily, this respect and amiability stayed throughout my training period.

My training journey began with the T-34 two-seat trainer, where I was assigned to a civilian male instructor pilot along with two other students. Our training consisted of both ground-based book training, covering the functions and operations of aircraft parts, and air-based training, where we got to experience the thrill of flying.

However, as I looked around, I noticed that all the instructors were white civilian males, and I couldn't recall seeing any black aircraft mechanics. Nonetheless, I focused on the task at hand and learned what it felt like to fly in three dimensions: up, down, and sideways. With each flight, I grew more confident, and by the end, I was required to make a solo flight within fourteen flying hours, consisting of seven flights. The experience was truly unforgettable.

I breezed through my ground training, but my flight performance was far from satisfactory. On my fifth and sixth flights, I was evaluated as lacking in pitch and bank control. The program was tough, as students would be washed out if they received three unsatisfactory evaluations or if they failed to solo on their seventh flight. Unfortunately, I knew that after my second unsatisfactory flight, I was likely to be included in the one-third of students who wouldn't make it through basic flight training.

But, by the grace of God, Christmas break arrived before my seventh flight. Upon my return, the commander gave each student two additional flights to reorient ourselves to what we had learned before the break. These flights wouldn't count against our required solo time, but they were essential in helping us avoid washing out.

Due to my previous unsatisfactory evaluations, I was required to fly with an Air Force pilot for an evaluation before my third unsatisfactory flight or before I was washed out of the program. During the pre-flight briefing, the Air Force pilot reviewed the problem areas identified by my civilian pilot and stressed that I needed to correct my pitch and bank control, maintain an altitude of 1100 feet in the traffic pattern through the downwind leg, and bank appropriately to make a rectangle traffic pattern over the ground with one side aligned with the runway, regardless of wind direction and speed.

I felt a mix of nervousness and determination as I prepared to prove myself and avoid being washed out of the program.

"I want you to correct pitch and bank, even if everything else goes to hell." My instructor commanded me.

I, along with my instructor, then conducted the pre-flight training.

With a confident yet nervous attitude, we conducted the pre-flight, took off, and burned down the fuel while performing confident maneuvers until we reached the traffic pattern. I had the memory of what my instructor said to me firmly ingrained in my mind and maintained an altitude of exactly 1,100 feet until it was time to begin our descent. I paralleled the runway, correcting for wind drift, as the tower called out, "Gear down and in the green."

I trusted the tower's instructions and set the flaps to one as we turned onto the final approach. Then I reduced the throttle, heard the horn begin to sound in my earphone, and saw the red light in the gear handle turn on.

However, I was so focused on pitch and back that neither the sound nor the light registered in my mind. My companion accused me of reaching for the gear lever and missing it, but I thought he would catch it when the tower said to check it. I thought he would have checked the gear indicator before telling the tower that the gear was down and in the green. I also assumed he would have checked the gear during the crosswind leg and again when the power was pulled back on the final leg. It wasn't until we began climbing to go around that he finally checked the gear indicator.

I knew I had failed my third and final evaluation, so I simply continued around the traffic pattern a second time with pitch and back controlled, dropping the gear properly, and lowering the flaps while reporting this to the tower once I had reviewed the appropriate indicators. Then I proceeded to land a greasy landing.

Once the plane was on the ground, I taxied it back to the parking apron. The indicator informed me that I had done exactly as he had told me.

"Correct pitch and bank if everything else goes to hell," I reminded him of his own words.

"You did just that. You could have killed us, destroyed this plane, or caused other damages." He spoke in a humorous tone.

"Yes, sir," I responded.

"You have learned an important lesson today." He said.

"Yes, sir," I replied.

"Do you think you can solo, enter the traffic pattern, and land?" He asked curiously.

"Yes, sir," I said with an even firmer tone.

"Take the plane up, enter the traffic pattern, land, taxi back in, and secure the plane. I will discuss your evaluation with you when you come back." He ordered, throwing the keys over to me.

The Air Force pilot evaluated me as he stepped out of the plane, wishing me a good flight.

While I taxied the aircraft to the edge of the runway, I called the tower for clearance for takeoff.

As I carefully guided the aircraft to the end of the runway, I felt a rush of excitement and anticipation. I called the tower for clearance for takeoff, eagerly awaiting their response. When the tower finally commanded *"hold for takeoff,"* I took a deep breath and meticulously rechecked all engine indicators and the flaps' lever position indicator, visually verifying their status.

Finally, the tower gave me the clearance for takeoff, and I was off to the skies! The plane lifted off, and I felt a thrill as I raised the gear and checked them, making sure they were all white. And when the flaps were up, I was overjoyed! I was flying solo, with no one looking over my shoulder or intimidating me from the back seat!

I was elated by the sound of the engine and the plane's responsive movements to every one of my commands. I climbed to the traffic pattern altitude and gracefully exited the pattern. I climbed above the traffic and leisurely flew around the airfield. My descent was smooth as I re-entered the traffic pattern, effortlessly navigating the downwind and crosswind legs before making a final approach with gear and flaps down. The plane touched down with grace, and I taxied back to the parking ramp, turning off the appropriate switches and circuit breakers.

Sitting there, I took a moment to admire my recent accomplishment and gave thanks to God for enabling me to do all things through Christ who strengthens me. The excitement was palpable as I felt confident that the evaluation had gone well and that I would be recommended to continue in the flight training program.

The debriefing and evaluation session ended on a high note, with a glowing recommendation from the evaluator. "You have the basic skills to build on and become an effective and efficient Air Force pilot," the evaluator announced.

I received favorable marks during my flight evaluations. Unfortunately, two of my classmates did not make it through basic flight school, but that's just how it is. Only the best and brightest are advanced to the next level.

As I moved on to the T-28 aircraft, I continued to hone my skills, becoming more confident with each maneuver, from loops and barrel rolls to navigation and night flying. The T-28 training was rigorous and demanding, but I used it as an invaluable learning opportunity, learning all the systems, procedures, and materials necessary to be a successful pilot. The training continued with oral navigation, radio/ADF training, and COR navigation.

I saw my success as a second chance at fulfilling my passion, and I was not going to let it slip this time. I am grateful to say that I completed my training without any incidents, emergencies, or accidents, and as a result, I was recommended for advanced flight training. It was thrilling; I was now one step closer to achieving my goal.

Chapter 3

With the advancing training levels, the thrill and joy of experiencing new things were aroused considerably in me. After my successful initial training, I was assigned to Webb Air Force Base, Big Spring, Texas. The task was to get advanced training in the T-33 jet. As in the previous training, all the trainees were grouped differently, each headed by an expert trainer. The ground training was a cakewalk for me, and I cruised effortlessly.

This time it was a different experience as we were flying jets, and things in the cockpit were happening faster. Moreover, landing with the T-33 initially seemed difficult, as I couldn't accurately determine the correct round-out technique. But gradually, my landings improved, and I could eventually land the plane smoothly on the runway. This was an achievement that came only with hard work, positivity, and lots of practice.

The training further included traffic pattern practices, confidence maneuvers, day and night cross-country flying, and learning about flying information and navigation. Though things were not easy for the first time for other students or me, I remember the gush of anguish and fear running through my bloodstream whenever another jet would come close to mine. It was a feeling unexplainable in words, but the moment could only be experienced. I used to maintain a significant distance between my and others' jets so as not to frighten myself even more, but that regrettably wasn't serving the purpose. My instructor kept commanding me by saying. *"Lieutenant, you're not flying formation... This is just two airplanes going in the same direction."*

Thus, I knew I had to buckle up and let my fears vanish because I was there to learn, not to fear. I assembled all my courage, bravery, and pluck. During my fourth and fifth days, I had all the assurance and buoyancy required by a wingman who was not only ready to fly but to fly stunningly, confidently, and hungrily. As a result, the instructor had to inform me several times to "back off" because I was too close to the jets.

That flight was an eye-opener for me, as I realized how great my confidence in myself was. The instructor's confidence in me wasn't that high; he doubted my abilities, but I, being myself, worked harder with more poise and self-confidence. Eventually, the instructor's and other students' belief in me developed, and he allowed us to fly in tight formation. We became the wingman while he flew the lead aircraft. The training continued in the same pattern for a few more days until some of us were washed out.

The training at Webb AFB happened in the panhandle of Texas during the winter, which made the drill harder. One winter day, I called the tower for landing instructions while returning from a flight. They permitted the landing and provided me with the necessary information regarding the weather.

Unluckily, the weather was bad, and the runway was covered in dust, rain, and mud, which made it hard to see. There was a severe crosswind from the right between 40 and 50 knots, adding fuel to the fire. The likelihood of meeting an accident, emergency, or mishap that could sometimes result in losing a student and plane flickered unintentionally in my mind and got me frozen for a few seconds. But by the grace of God and an apt landing, I landed safe and sound.

Another incident happened on a day when I was all set to fly high. I was rolling smartly in the air, and as I lifted off, I heard a dire scream from one of the wing planes, *"Oh shoot, my engine... it's blown."* The student shouted frightfully and continued, *"I am losing power!"*

The student ahead of me had blown his engine and shouted for help. Within a blink of an eye, I saw the lethal black smoke from his plane's engine; it was a terrible sight. Afterward, he turned his plane down towards the fields and descended haphazardly. As he didn't get enough time to determine a suitable plot for landing, he crashed and landed outside a small housing area. I could see the crashed plane covered with black smoke from the sky, but there was no fire.

A man was observing the calamitous situation; he immediately ran inside his house to get an axe to cut the aluminum. He helped the student pilot get out of the plane. The student pilot appeared to have minor injuries and was fortunately saved from the plane crash. I was fascinated by the man's kindness and efforts—he saved the pilot without thinking about the danger. Subsequently, I reported back to the tower about the mishap and asked for the rescue teams. Later, I headed back to the training area to practice my assigned maneuvers for the day.

The training included accidents and mishaps, but more than that, it brought tears and unfulfilled dreams to many students. The students who didn't give an up-to-the-mark performance were washed out at the program level. To narrate an instance, a student pilot performed numerous spins over his girlfriend's house to impress her. Though he made great efforts, the ending wasn't happy. He crashed his aircraft near her house, resulting in his death and destroying the aircraft.

From the training and understanding I developed from others' experiences, I recognized that the foremost reasons behind accidents and crashes were lack of judgment, human error, and horseplay. As a result, I developed the habit of learning the capabilities and designs of my assigned aircraft. Then, with my limited experience and skills, I would figure out what I could do with the plane.

At last, those students who followed the rules, safety procedures, and warnings and were proficient in flying were recommended for graduation. They received wings certifying them as U.S. Air Force pilots, including me.

I could still vividly reminisce about every moment of the memorable day when I received my dearest wing, the wing that I received after great struggle, hard work, and continued long hours of practice. That beautiful moment was indubitably the most exhilarating and joyful time in my military career. It was an achievement that I felt I could never acquire, but I did it. I remember my heart pounding differently that day and my soul being filled with gratitude, contentment, and an earnest desire to help the world with my skills. The moment the honorary wing was pinned on my uniform's left side, I could feel the pressure and responsibility to strive harder to protect humanity.

Moreover, the wing helped us gain respect and acceptance into the Air Force elite flying club, which excited everyone. We were given an aeronautical rating and were told that these wings indicated that we were no longer student pilots but real 'PILOTS' in capital letters. The moment itself was extraordinary and made me feel over the moon. I could feel my heart pounding with pride and gratitude. The wing wasn't limited to my uniform only; it got profoundly engraved in my heart, reminding me every time to fly as high as I could with my soul and the plane's wings flaunting fluently in the air.

However, that accomplishment could have never existed without my instructors' indefatigable efforts and patience. I will always remember my one sincere and honest instructor, to whom we would frighten half to death many times.

After each thrilling flight, he used to say, *"Flying is for birds; I will get myself a desk job and give up training students before one of you kills me."*

***

As the days passed, I was reassigned from air training command to tactical air command, which was a huge accomplishment. I was initially commanded to become proficient in the F-86 Sabra at William Air Force Base, Arizona, during the tactical air command.

The day we first checked out of our F-86 marked the official beginning of our training to become ready for any combat. The training included learning ground tactics using guns and rockets. It included tasks such as dive bombing, toss bombing, and evading low-level navigation. In addition, at some advanced level, we had to practice high-level navigation, air-to-air combat training, formation flying, and squadron protection training. Moreover, we practiced heavily on our gun and rocket ranges to enhance our skills.

Once, during our dive-bombing range practices, a few Chinese pilots were among the trainees too. While I made my dive bomb run after releasing and pulling it up, I recognized another pilot following me and doing the same practice successfully. After us, there came another pilot who began his dive but was unable to pull the bomb quickly. I heard the range officer shouting to pull up the bomb rapidly. Afterward, I returned to the Base and never knew whether he could do it.

Another training day was initiated, and one of our flight leaders planned a cross-country three-leg round-robin to Albuquerque, N.M. The plan wasn't limited to flying and returning but included an overnight stay in El Paso, Texas, before returning to William Air Base. Initially, our flight leader climbed his plane and leveled off at cruising altitude. Suddenly, his navigation system became inoperative.

"My navigation system isn't working. Give me heading during the first leg, Lt. George Burns." The flight leader commanded the second lieutenant.

After a long flight filled with uncertainty, we could successfully and soundly land at the air base located in Albuquerque. After a peaceful landing, the flight leader acknowledged the crew chief in writing about the problem.

After concluding our scrumptious breakfast, the next morning, we checked our flight plan for the next two legs. Along with it, we monitored the weather conditions and established a workable flight plan. As we entered the cockpit and examined all the navigational equipment and radios, the tower granted us permission to depart. Afterward, we taxied ourselves into the runway and joined in formation to the cruising altitude after exiting the traffic pattern.

We breezed through the clouds and toward the VFR tower, maneuvering it on top of the visual flight rules and then over the top of the clouds in the sky. Suddenly, a strange thing happened. Though the flight leader's navigation system was fixed earlier, it began to show erroneous indications. When the flight leader figured out the situation, his radio system collapsed. Consequently, he couldn't communicate with the ground staff or us.

As we figured out the problem, we communicated through hand signals. Our flight commander commanded Lt. George Burns to lead the squadron as his equipment was in good condition. At the same time, the other wingman and I were also facing problems with the navigation system. But we had learned from our practices that as long as one of the navigation systems is working in the squadron, no problem exists for anyone. Thus, our flight continued to fly smoothly.

We proceeded to report our information related to location altitude and estimated time of heading and arriving at Williams to El Paso Center before another happening occurred in this eventful flight. Our new leader, George Burns, reported haphazardly that he had run out of oxygen and had to land immediately. After informing us, he descended his plane speedily. As the flight leader didn't have a working radio, he didn't realize the reason behind our speedy landing, nor was he familiar with the speed.

To identify him with our sudden action, we used hand signals. Fortunately, the hand signals worked in our favor, and we descended safely. But another problem existed—a fuel shortage to reach William AFB. Since we were flying at a low altitude, we lacked the fuel to reach the home station. Therefore, we headed back to El Paso. When we reached the Air Force base, we hastily received permission for an emergency landing. By this time, the flight leader took the lead again. To our further astonishment, we didn't know that the AFB was closed due to a repair operation, but our flight leader knew.

Since it was an emergency stop, the tower provided us with the much-needed clearance even though the runway was closed for official traffic. Suddenly, I realized that I was left with only enough fuel for one approach and couldn't reach El Paso International Airport. I informed the other two pilots about my situation and the urgent need to land or bail out. Considering my situation, my fellow pilots could only envision me crashing into a piece of heavy equipment and getting killed due to an accident.

Since the runway was closed, I might have hit my plane with a heavy object. To fuel the fire, I had zero knowledge regarding the runway length or surface. But I knew that I had to do this. Hence, I slowed down my aircraft, and gradually it touched down on the runway. I keenly observed the runway ahead of me. In the meantime, the tower informed me about the next taxiway two or three thousand feet further from me. Thus, I added power to shorten my time as I ran out of fuel. The other pilots and the flight leader continued to follow me.

In a few moments, all of us were on the runway, doing our best to deliver a safe landing. While we were still on the runway, the base commander in the tower questioned our landing on a closed runway. I explained to him about the emergency because I was the pilot who touched down first. Afterward, we taxied our planes into the ramp and parked them successfully.

Once we came back, the base commander's curiosity, or perhaps his agitation, didn't lessen, and he questioned our landing on the closed runway.

"Colonel, what would you have done if you had three student pilots with various emergencies, including the planes? All four aircraft had emergencies of some type or another, Colonel." Our flight leader enunciated at the base commander.

The stringent reply made the base commander speechless, and he left without responding. However, he took the flight leader alongside him to his office. There, they called the squadron commander of William AFB too. Furthermore, when we arrived back at the Base, we learned that the incident news had already been spread over the station like fire.

The first incident didn't deter us, and despite being subsonic, we took the F-86 Sabre tactical fighter through the second barrier on our next practice. This was done to become a member of the Mark Buster Club.

With that, my combat training came to an end. All the successful pilots became certified combat-ready, including me. Now that one step had concluded, we started awaiting orders to be assigned to a Tactical Air Command.

A few days after the graduation ceremony, we were informed that the strategic air command (SAC) required a squadron of good, polished pilots. All the selected pilots would be reassigned to SAC to be trained as copilots in SAC aircraft, i.e., 135s, B-47s, and B-52s. In contrast, we all wanted to stay in the Tactical Air Command and continue training as fighter pilots.

Chapter 4

In the ensuing days, the complete atmosphere of William Air Base was encircled by a single debate of which squadron would be selected for the SAC versus who would continue with the TAC. It was a subject that hooked everyone, including me, and we continued waiting for the results anxiously. Eventually, the much-awaited results were announced, which surprised me.

The squadron I belonged to got selected for the SAC without us knowing any reason other than that the SAC urgently needed highly trained and proficient pilots. After the results, we immediately got ourselves prepared for the new beginning.

Being in SAC, we were advised to choose an aircraft and desired duty station according to our ranking in the squadron. Thus, I chose the B-52G aircraft and received my first assignment at Seymour Johnson Air Force Base in Goldsboro, North Carolina, near my hometown, Maysville, N.C. Before reporting to Seymour Johnson, I was sent to B-52G weapons and aircraft school and their survival school to gain knowledge of and become familiar with my aircraft. As I wasn't assigned to Seymour Johnson as a crew member, I couldn't enjoy the benefits of SAC crew training at Coastal AFB, Georgia.

While in San Antonio, Texas, at Lakeland AFB, I bought myself a pre-loved light green 1956 Chevrolet V8 power pack with a four-door white hard top. This car had my heart, as it was my very first car with my name on the title. Undeniably, it was a beautiful car that I loved and cared immensely for. It stayed with me throughout my pilot training tenure.

Returning from survival school in 1958, I came across a secondhand 1958 Cadillac at a Fort Worth, Texas, car dealership. Its appearance made it a special sixties car. It had wide chrome running from the back door, across the rear fender, to the bumper, and a four-door hard top. It was white with an attractive blue interior. Honestly, it was the most elegant automobile I had ever witnessed. Thus, I couldn't resist, so I traded my Chevrolet for the Cadillac.

I enjoyed the car dealership experience at Fort Worth with a white marine who was going to Alabama. After getting comfortable in my new Cadillac, the white Marine and I headed toward Louisiana, Mississippi, Alabama, and North Carolina. We enjoyed the journey as everything was going well and smoothly. But the moment we reached Alabama and the white Marine left, the trouble started. The problem emerged when I stopped by the gas station for the first time.

It was 01:00 am when I stopped at a small service station to fill up the gas tank. A service station attendant came out to pump gas as my car approached the station. After placing the nozzle in the tank, the attendant returned to the station and talked with his other two white males. After a while, all three males came out and viewed my car. When the meter approached six dollars, I asked the attendant to halt fueling the tank. While I was cranking up the car, I was interrupted by one of the men.

"Where did you steal this car from?" He inquired nosily.

"That's my father's car. He owns a couple of oil wells." I immediately replied confidently. "You can check the Texas plates if you do not believe me," I added.

As one boy walked toward the back to check the license plates, I handed over six dollars to the attendant. I realized that the other white person approached his pickup truck to get something like a rod or baton. Thus, I swiftly pulled off and left the service station, sprinting. Without pausing for a minute, I drove to a big station with many white and black people coming and going. I filled my tank at that station and did the same throughout my journey.

Fortunately, I concluded my journey without incident and reported to Seymour Johnson for duty. Since I wasn't sufficiently trained for the B-52G, I couldn't become a full and active crew member. Thus, I spent most of my time flying the T-33, orienting newly assigned pilots to the area.

In the span of three to four months, I was commanded to fly as a third pilot in different crews to receive significant training opportunities in the B-52G aircraft. In reality, I didn't get ample control time because the training flight was so demanding for the regular crew members. This practice continued for a while.

Back home, I learned that my brother had wrecked my NSU Prinz, a small car with two-cylinder engines—a German thing. The car was totaled and couldn't be repaired. Thus, I bought another one that stayed in the parking lot most of the time. After eighteen months, I sold the second car to the junkyard and purchased a used Chevrolet Corvair.

The Base where I was stationed was less than 100 miles from Belgrade, North Carolina. Belgrade is the community where my family lived, and where I grew up. My eldest brother had moved to New York City for better wages, and my wife and daughter lived with my parent. them. The benefit of living near my hometown made it convient for me to spend weekends at home and return to Seymour Johnson on Monday morning.

Moreover, my Tuesday, Thursday, and Friday nights were spent at home, with Monday and Wednesday staying in my temporary BBQ room. Over time, I acquired full and active membership in Seymour Johnson's officer club, which I maintained and utilized attentively.

In 1960, I faced a maintenance problem with my second car, an NSU Prinz; therefore, I had to drive my 1958 Cadillac to work. One day, I dropped by a service station east of Seymour Johnson to pump gas in the car. Though I was wearing an Air Force uniform, the service station owner refused to provide fuel to my car. When I inquired about the reason, he only replied, "I cannot sell you any gasoline."

After hearing his rude response, I returned to my car without inquiring further. Suddenly, I heard another service station attendant calling out, saying he would sell me all the gas I wanted. Ironically, both gas stations were owned and operated by whites. One refused, and the other amazed me with his positive response. From that day on, I used his service station for pumping gas into my car, particularly when driving my Cadillac.

When I drove the Cadillac to work for the second or third time, a first lieutenant who was an Electronics Warfare Officer (EWO) asked a strange question.

"Lt. Mattocks, how can you afford two cars on a lieutenant's pay?" He asked inquisitively.

"What is your per-month club bill?" I asked politely but with grace.

"It ranges between three hundred and three hundred fifty dollars a month." He stated.

"Mine was between one hundred and one hundred and twenty-five dollars," I responded amusingly. "I do not drink or dance in the clubs, which became the reason for my lower club bills. I wisely utilized the saved money to buy another car for myself." I added.

"Oh!" He sighed.

"The monthly payments for a Cadillac are one hundred twenty-eight dollars and fifty-eight cents," I informed him, which impressed him.

Just as the Second Lieutenant and I were conversing about my expenses and new car, the lieutenant's crew commander appeared behind us. He heard everything we discussed but stayed silent throughout our discussion. When we eventually looked around and caught him standing, he spoke.

"Lieutenant Mattocks, are you getting enough flying time at the control during your flights?" the commander inquired sternly.

"I receive little flight time in the right seat with different crews," I answered honestly.

"Would you like to fly with us on my crew?" He added. "I will provide enough time in the B-52G aircraft."

I couldn't believe my ears. As sincerely as he spoke, it excited me, and of course I was thrilled. I had been waiting for this, and now that I had finally received the opportunity, I couldn't wait to start it.

The lieutenant commander informed the operations officer about my insufficient training time at the controls in the right seat. He told them that he could provide me with adequate time and keep a check on me from the right seat. In addition, I, too, had a conversation with the operations officer where I told them about my concerns related to training requirements and needs. Considering my request, the operations crew asked for my permission to be assigned to the commander's crew, which I affirmed at the earliest.

Consequently, I was assigned to his crew and my performance evaluation would be presented in approximately twenty-eight days.

Prior to my performance evaluation, I flew three times with my new crew. However, contrary to what I anticipated before joining this crew, I received comparatively less time at the controls and right seats than the random crews I was previously flying with. After each flight, the commander promised to give me more time on the next flight, but his promise was never fulfilled.

Afterward, when the performance evaluation phase arrived, he prepared a report based on my original assessment and rated me unsatisfactory. I never saw the report, nor did the operations officer; however, I learned about it from another crew member. The unsatisfactory ratings had to be justified with factual performance data or any incidents in the evaluation report. But the commander didn't provide substantial proof and said I didn't support the Officer Club.

The operation officer immediately rejected his evaluation report by rejecting the justification provided by the crew commander. He then ordered him to develop a new evaluation report. The new evaluation report had every column marked as 'satisfactory,' because both of us knew that a satisfactory evaluation couldn't be challenged and did not require any justification. It was disappointing for someone like me, who had always secured 'excellent' ratings in the previous assessments. I knew that I wasn't evaluated based on my actual performance but rather because the crew commander wanted to take control of me and exercise his manipulative racism on me.

Since the crew commander was a Lt. Colonel, he had a position to affect my career significantly. Thus, I requested to be reassigned to another crew. I was familiar with racism then; therefore, I sought to think for a couple of days before giving the operation officers my preferred crew commander's name. After contemplating for days, I asked to be assigned to Major Tullock's crew.

Besides that, I challenged the satisfactory evaluation rating through the chain of command to the Pentagon. I objected to the insufficient timeframe of 28 days and claimed that my evaluation wasn't derived from my original performance. As expected, my appeal was denied on every step, with the justification that a crew commander has a right to rate based on his observations. Moreover, the satisfactory rating couldn't be challenged. However, each one of us was well familiar with his real motives.

The evaluation graph of my entire flying career shows a straight line representing all the excellent ratings but suddenly shows a drastic drop in four lines. Then they go back up to excellent ratings and continue with the straight line. Whenever someone looks at my report, it appears as if something tragic was committed by me, perhaps a murder or the destruction of military property worth millions of dollars.

The declining ratings constantly troubled me, and I did everything possible to correct my record, but to no avail. Racism was inevitable, and at that moment, I realized how drastically racism could deteriorate or even end my Air Force career. Still, I remained optimistic, hoping that someone would have the guts to correct my record, but sadly, no one came forth.

Soon, I realized that it was easier for me to accept my satisfactory rating instead of confronting the deep ascribed roots of racism and systematic discrimination. The same system coerced capable military officers to resign from military service, and those who did not were forced out of the services. Similarly, due to this brutal practice against me, my military career was destined to end in two or three years.

The operation officer, Major Tulloch, and all the white crew members treated me respectfully and with dignity during my time at Seymour Johnson. Most importantly, my performance evaluation was drafted based on my actual performance, and I continued flying with Major Tulloch. Unexpectedly, he gave me ample time on the controls and the right seat.

On a cold January morning in January 1961, Major Tulloch's crew prepared for a 24-hour combat-loaded, airborne alert mission. I spent two hours preparing myself with emergency procedures in the B-52G simulator. Everything was great, except it was difficult for me to get the simulator out of a spin.

The crew, plus me and one additional person, were to fly with the crew. They were Major Walker S. Tulloch, pilot/aircraft commander, Captain Richard W. Radin, copilot, 1st LT. William R. Wilson, Electronics war force officer, Captain Paul E. Brown, navigator, Major Eugene Shelton, Radar Navigator, TSGT Francis R. Barnish, Gunnery, Major Eugene H. Richards, Instructor Electronics war force Officer, and 1/lt. Adam C. Mattocks, the 3rd pilot, who occupied the instructor pilot seat.

January 23, 1961

By 0845 EST, we had completed all the pre-flight inspections and monitoring and had entered the aircraft. Someone asked me to wear my parachute snug and tight without specifying the reason. It sounded unusual to me on a 24-hour-long mission, but I obeyed the orders and tightened my parachute accordingly. I remained wearing the parachute throughout the flight.

After Major Tulloch received clearance for takeoff, we concluded a successful takeoff of our aircraft on accurate time. At 1056 EST, our flight was officially in the air at a normal cruising altitude. Everything was smooth, and we air-refueled the aircraft twice.

However, suddenly we realized a leak in the number four tank. The Boom Operator of the KC-135 reported a sheet of fuel about 15 feet wide and 20 to 50 feet long was coming out of the right-wing underneath the #3 pod. Within a few minutes, tank number four had lost all the fuel stored inside it. In the nick of time, Tank 04 fuel indicator changed from twenty-three thousand pounds of JP-4 fuel to zero. Due to this, the aircraft's left wing became twenty thousand pounds heavier than the right wing. But the disaster didn't stop there.

Unexpectedly, tank number three started to leak, but at a slower rate. The laterally imbalanced flight and the leaking flight tanks weren't our only worries; there was also the potential fire hazard and explosion that could be ignited from the leaking tanks. Everyone was engaged in finding a solution to the sudden problem. Suddenly, the cockpit crew decided to stop engines five and six to avoid the possible fire hazard.

This approach may instantly reduce the fire risk, but I could see that it will lead to further emergencies. As a result, we might lose a hydraulic pump and an electrical motor. Then, we provided electric current to the moving parts after rechecking the circuit breakers and rerouting both hydraulic pressures to serve all hydraulic moving parts. To ensure that all moving parts responded properly, the copilot and I checked to see if all switches and circuit breakers were either in or out, on or off.

After engines 5 and 6 were closed, the remaining six engines were fed from the first and second main fuel tanks. The cockpit crew constantly watched the leaking tank and the tanks used to feed the engines. They tried to bring the aircraft back into lateral balance.

After a few minutes into the emergency, it was determined that the #4 main tank was empty, the #3 main tank was approximately half empty, and the right external fuel tank was down by one-third. With time, things were getting worse for us. As the cockpit crew was incessantly in touch with the command post, the aircraft commander requested a change in his flight plan. Moreover, he needed clearance to proceed to a point ten miles offshore, southeast of Camp Lejeune and Camp Fear. We orbited at an altitude of 29,000 feet for about two hours, burning fuel from the left-wing tanks to reach the desired landing weight.

We contacted the Raleigh-Durham tower through Seymour Johnson

Approach Control.

"Seymour Johnson Approach Control, this is keep one nine. We are proceeding directly from Wilmington to Seymour on nine zero-flight levels. We are descending through two zero-point five at present. Roger!" We conversed.

"Keep one nine! Seymour Johnson, the weather is clear. Visibility is ten miles. Wind southwest at six. Altimeter is two nine six." They informed and continued, "Landing on runway two six at Seymour Johnson, and you can turn on radar vector to runway two six. Will you be able to make a turn for radar identification?"

"That's affirmative." Keep One Nine affirmed.

"Keep one nine-this. This is Seymour Johnson, Approach Control. Squawk three normal for Seymour, GCA owner. Roger!" Seymour Johnson informed.

"Keep one nine is squawking three normal." We communicated the controls.

Seymour from Approach Control asked, "Where are you heading now?"

Keep One Nine responded, "We're heading three four degrees."

"Keep one Nine, we have radar contact with you. Forty miles south of Seymour Johnson, you are heading three four zero degrees. Descend and maintain two thousand, and this will be a radar vector to the GCA final approach course landing runway two-six over." They explained.

"Approach this is keep one nine. Standby, we're going to let our gear down first. Roger." We updated.

"Keep one nine, advise me when you start your descent." Seymour Approach Control requested.

After a while, Seymour Johnson Approach Control asked again, ""Keep one nine, have you started your descent yet?" "

"Negative approach. I am putting the gear down in a special way, and

I'll begin descending as soon as I get the gear down." We notified.

Simultaneously, the aircraft commander commanded one of the navigators to check the condition of the wheels. As per his reporting, all the equipment and instruments, including wheel wells and bomb bays, were submerged in fuel, creating an additional risk of hazard. This put extra responsibility on the cockpit crew to gear down without igniting the fuel in the wheel well. In addition, we had two hydrogen bombs in the megaton range drenched with JP-4 fuel, creating a major dilemma.

Eventually, the cockpit crew decided to freely let the gears fall into place while relying on gravity to make them fall downward. They pulled all the circuit breakers and made sure all the switches were off. Though we had a feeling that the gears would fall downward, we had zero expectations of them being locked. This again posed a potential hazard because if they weren't locked, the heavy load would collapse the wheels.

After a few minutes, the aircraft commander repeatedly commanded someone to check the gear. The navigator said the gears were downward but he couldn't see if they were locked. Thus, the risk of the explosion didn't fade away, nor did our agitation.

To verify that all the gears were down and locked, we were supposed to turn on the circuit breaker and switches that could cause an explosion; this fact had everyone subdued. However, we had to do everything necessary for our survival. Thus, we held our breath and pushed in the circuit breakers, and the switches were turned on. Consequently, all the gears and indicators were geared down and locked.

The news brought a ray of hope, and we took a deep breath. However, we had overcome a major hurdle, and another one awaited us. Considering the potential structural damage, would this aircraft operate and be controlled at slow speeds, such as landing speed?

Before then, we had descended to 10,000 feet. We had to slow the plane down and gradually lower the flaps because the gear was not securely in place. Early on during the incident, we were told there was no significant structural damage. The plane had normally been operating for a couple of hours, so we mentally estimated that we would be landing in fifteen or twenty minutes.

The copilot adjusted the flaps to the initial increment of degrees. I once again verified all the circuit breakers on the right, left, and top load central panels. Sitting in the instructor pilot seat, I could observe and assist the rest of the cockpit crew.

On the upper deck were five crew members, with three in the cockpit. The cockpit included Major Tullock in the left ejection seat, Captain Rordin in the right ejection seat, and me in the instructor pilot stationary seat, whereas two others were in the EWO's and Gunner Department ejection seats. Everyone in the ejection seats had to eject the occupant upward to egress the plane. The pilot occupying the instructor pilot seat must walk down a ladder to the bottom or lower deck and bail out the navigator hatch.

The sequence of crew members' egress was planned in a secure and organized manner. Due to the height and length of the vertical and horizontal stabilizers, no one could jump very high. Therefore, it was recommended that no one try to jump from the top. It was decided that the navigator would rotate his levers and blow his hatch downward. Then he would eject downward, leaving an opening for the next person in the lower deck to bail out. All the crew members would follow the same opening in the top deck.

The radar navigator informed the aircraft commander after both the navigators and the pilot left the plane, and then he ejected too. Afterward, the Gunner, EWO, copilot, and aircraft commander were prepared to egress in their pre-planned order. On the other hand, I knew that I had to get to the bottom deck to bail out, thanks to my knowledge of bailout procedures. Thus, I observed all instruments and indicators while they were descending with the gear extended down.

"Keep One Nine, this. This is Seymour Johnson, Approach Control. Turn right, heading zero two zero. You are now twenty-eight miles south of Seymour Johnson." Seymour Johnson informed us.

"I understand. Steer zero two zero." We replied.

"That's affirmative. Turn right, heading zero two zero." The Approach Control announced.

Subsequently, I checked all the indicators and engines (1st, 2nd, 3rd, 4th, 7th, and 8th). All of them were normal. Also, engines 5th and 6th were shut down previously. I noticed that the plane was moving forwarding in a right-turn position.

"Keep one nine, this is Seymour Johnson Approach Control. Turn left, heading three six zero. THREE SIX ZERO. You are now twenty miles southeast of Seymour Johnson over!"

Keep one nine replied, "We're turning left to three six zero. The command post wants me to hold at ten thousand feet. I'll have to see what they want. I must hold here."

"Keep one nine, I understand. You are going to maintain ten thousand feet until further advised. Is that correct?" They inquired.

"That's affirmative. I'll call you back." Keep One Nine responded.

Seymour Johnson from Approach Control replied, "Roger!"

""Keep one nine, keep one nine," They pronounced. "This is Seymour Approach Control. Traffic is eleven o'clock, seven miles southwest bound over.

"Roger!" Keep one nine replied.

"Keep one nine. This is Seymour, Approach Control. Turn left, heading two seven zero."

Keep one nine asked, "Seymour, approach, did you receive?"

Seymour from Approach Control answered, "I want to check in on this airplane. I'll maintain ten thousand feet and hold this heading three two zero. Roger."

"This is Seymour, Approach Control. I understand you will continue heading three two zero and maintaining ten thousand. We'll advise

Washington Center that you're leaving our high-altitude area and currently crossing the Washington Center airway. We'll advise them." Seymour Approach notified.

"Whatever you want. Turn me in whatever direction you want me to go. Roger," I responded.

"Keep one nine. Washington Center requested us to get you in our high-altitude area and keep you in that area away from their traffic." Seymour informed us.

Keep one nine responded, "Roger."

Seymour said, "Now turn left heading to two six zero. Roger."

"This is Keep one nine. We have left to two six zero." We apprised.

Despite the controls being toward the left, I realized the aircraft was still moving towards a slight right turn. This difficult situation wasn't unusual because B-52 had lagged in the control movements. I turned back towards the console, and regardless of full left controls, we couldn't get the right wing up. Therefore. I diverted my entire focus to controlling the aircraft.

Suddenly, our plane began to roll slightly to the right. Instantly, the aircraft commander ordered the copilots to pull back engines 1 and 2. Both pilots fought hard to keep the plane from rolling. As my seat was near the throttles, I pulled back the two engines. Fortunately, it slowed down the rolling of the plane.

Afterward, the aircraft commander commanded to push engine numbers 7 and 8 to activate their power. As we were losing airspeed, the pilot nosed down. At that moment, we were traveling at approximately thirty degrees' bank to the right, nose down, picking up speed. However, the roll to the right momentarily stopped toward the front of the plane but not at the rear.

While I was flying backward and had no idea how I got there, I was aware that it was something stronger and more powerful than I was.

CONTINUED…

When I looked at the cockpit ahead of me, I saw the copilot rotating his ejection seat triggers and, consequently, his hatch jettisoned. Suddenly, his steering control moved forward and in an abrupt direction. He then tightly squeezed the trigger and the seat.

At this moment, I realized that a very short time had passed, but it felt like the pilot had been ejecting for a long time. Normally, the cockpit crew allowed the lower deck crew to eject or bail out approximately three to seven seconds before they would jettison the upper hatch. After looking at the copilot eject, I learned it had only been a short time since the plane started spinning.

Once my debate with myself ended, I realized that the copilot was still ejecting and the positive "G" forces were reducing rampantly. Suddenly, the aircraft commander turned around to look at me. I could sense the hopeless expression on his face, as if he had realized that regardless of his struggles, he couldn't control the plane any longer.

He rotated the handle that was fixed on the armrest, and subsequently, he jettisoned his hatch. Afterward, the aircraft commander pulled the trigger along with his seat and ejected from the plane.

When I watched the copilot eject, I murmured, "Mattocks, you and the plane are still spiraling downward. You are still unable to walk to the ladder downstairs and bail out before it hits the ground."

I shook my head, disappointed, and continued, "The copilot hatch is open, and no one in the plane is spinning to the right. If I jump for the copilot hatch, the hatch will rotate from me when I am in midair. Thus, I would miss the hatch."

However, when I saw the aircraft commander ejecting, I felt that if I had followed the aircraft commander, I would have gotten out successfully. But before I could join him, the aircraft commander ejected, leaving me alone on the plane.

I became scared and screamed, "Oh God, I am going down all by myself and will die alone," I said this because I was assured that everyone had gotten out.

Without wasting any time, I jumped from my location. . While I was in midair, between the floor and the top of the plane, the cockpit rotated. But when I arrived at the hatch, I could see the cockpit before me. I rested my hands on each side to pull myself through. However, I realized there wasn't any need to pull, because something else pushed me out of the opening. I wasn't sure if it were an explosion erupting inside the plane or whatever. I knew that neither the plane nor the situation was in our control.

Even after safely jumping through the aircraft commander's hatch, I knew I was in imminent danger. I knew I must carefully pass between the horizontal and vertical stableness while this huge planespins out of control. Subsequently, as I went through the top hatch, I balled up in as small a knot as I could, waiting to get hit by the horizontal or vertical stabilizers.

Surprisingly, another unexpected incident occurred.

As I was pushed out of the hatch, all balled up for safety, I was unable to feel any movement. It seemed as if I were suspended in space. I couldn't even feel the wind passing over, under and all around me. Within a few moments, I eventually felt myself falling through the air. However, I was still unaware of whether I had cleared the plane. That is when I began counting down.

"One thousand and one. One thousand and two. One thousand and three."

As I fell, I pulled my "D" ring and monitored the process intensely. I could feel the parachute pulling on the canopy. While anxiously waiting for the parachute to pull the canopy out, I said, "Oh God, you brought me out of this breaking-up plane, and now, I need my chute to work."

Suddenly, the canopy began slowing my falling. I immediately straighten out under my parachute. When I looked up, a tragic sight, to be hold, caught my attention. My canopy collapsed due to the shock wave caused by the explosion from the plane that housed the crew including me a few minutes earlier..

"Oh Lord, I have a streamer," I said immediately.

To my astonishment, as if someone was were listening, my canopy blossomed completely at that time, demonstrating that my parachute had started functioning perfectly. However, my air dilemma was still real. I could see the burning chunks of the plane flying through the air and I could visualize pieces burning through me. I again said to myself,

"Adam, the Lord God made you a way out of no way to egress from this falling plane, protected you from all protruding parts of the plane's body, secured your safety in the parachute that is now about to lose its canopy or get it cut loose by these burning pieces as they come by with fire and smokes," I said to myself and felt grateful. My heart was brightened with God's blessing.

As I floated uninhibited toward the earth, I glanced over the beautifully clear and bright moon that had lit the night. The moon hovered above the trees, making the scenario more serene and eye-catching. The entire air of the region was quiet and peaceful.

When I looked up, I saw four more parachutes coming downward. Assuming them to be the aircraft commander, the copilot, the navigator, and the instructor navigator.

Afterward, I diverted my attention toward the ground because the landing time had finally arrived. However, when I looked down, the whole earth appeared to be on fire. As the fire burned my eyes, I couldn't say, "Oh God, you have miraculously delivered me to this moment, and now I will land in this fuel and fire." I knew there was no way I could land on this fire and get out of it alive.

"Lord, I am totally and completely in your hands." I cried.

I looked up at the stars to relax my restless mind and let out the fear. Then, I looked down and witnessed God's miracle. The miracle happening beneath me astounded me, and I was pleased. I felt myself moving backward from the fire. As God's miracle took me away from the fire, tears began to roll out of my eyes.

I could hear, as clear as day, my mother and grandmother's prayers at that moment. Their words kept resonating in my ears. "Oh God, take care of my children, protect them, and keep them safely in your care."

I was being blown by the wind here and there. At one point, I would float over the burning plane; however, the next moment, I was over the fields. As I passed over the fields, I prepared my parachute for landing on the field. Similarly, when I was passing over the woods, I would prepare for a parachute landing in the woods. This continued for a while.

As I was drifting over this field, suddenly, I looked over my left shoulder and saw the trees again. Since it was night, my depth perception was off, and I could not estimate how high I was above the ground. I pulled my chute to stop my backward movement to land in this field. Afterward, I began falling rapidly. Hence, I released the cords of the chute. Fortunately, it was enough to stop my backward movement.

I observed the trees and moon setting in the West from a distance. The moon was above the tree top. From this, I estimated I was about two to three hundred feet above the ground. Then, I prepared myself for landing in this field with a forward roll.

However, as I hit the ground planning a forward roll, I sank and did not bounce during landing. Little did I know, I was landing on the back side of a farmhouse. The farmhouse had a breezeway between the main part of the house and the kitchen.

After standing on my feet, I pulled the oxygen mask from over my face, picked up my parachute, and rolled up. I cautiously but happily walked toward the breezeway that had a porch-like structure. As I stepped up on the breezeway, I saw some people standing in awe, looking shockingly at the burning plane.

I became an unusual sight for them as I was dressed in a flight suit with my helmet on. Most of them were fascinated by my appearance. To make them comfortable, I initiated the conversation.

"Don't be afraid! I have just bailed out of that burning plane." I said to them.

Later, I inquired if either could drive me to Seymour Johnson Air Force Base. Fortunately, a black family invited me into their home.

After I approached their home, the family and I had a pleasant conversation for a little while.

"If anyone can take me to Seymour Johnson Air Force Base," I asked again, as I was anxious and wanted to return.

The mother said, "My son has gone to the store and will return in a few minutes."

The black family explained everything they had heard, felt, and seen as the burning plane approached their house. They heard the subsequent explosion after the spiraling plane hit the ground.

"We experienced control problems in addition to the current emergency while putting down the flaps. The plane was uncontrollable, and we had to bail out." I explained to them.

Within ten to fifteen minutes, her son returned from the store and took me to Seymour Johnson Air Force Base. When I reached the entrance, I got out of his car. When I tried to enter the Air Force Base, the Air Force Police didn't allow me to enter because I had lost my identification during the bailout.

"You have an unauthorized military property (a parachute)." A policeman said.

Due to the crash and sudden bailout, all of the pockets on my chest, arms, thighs, and legs were gone. I didn't have a single thing that would identify me.

A few minutes later, another crew member from the burning plane arrived at the gate. Surprisingly, even he didn't have any identification with him. Now, both of us were held at the gate. Later, we asked the Air Force Police to call base operation to ask the operation officer if he had heard that a B-52 was down.

The police made the call to the operations officer. The operations officer said he knew nothing about a B-52 being down. As the other crew member and I talked, we decided to have the Air Force Police call the base operations officer again.

However, this time we told the police officer to ask him, "Did a B-52 take off yesterday morning at 1056 EST? Call sign - keep one niner. With a crew of eight, including Major Tulloch, Capt. Rardin, Lt. Wilson, Capt. Brown, Maj Sheltom, TSGT Barnish, Major Richards, and Lt. Mattocks."

After this thorough and detailed question, the operations officer responded, "yes."

After that, we asked the Air Force police to inform him that he had Captain Rardin and Lt. Mattocks at the gate.

Within minutes, Air Force police care arrived at the gate and took us to the hospital.

The doctors at the hospital treated us on a priority basis, and I found out that I had a bruise on my right thigh. After treatment, I was put in a secured room where officials came and asked different questions.

"Lt. Mattocks, how did you get out?" It was the most frequently asked question.

"I bailed out of the aircraft commander's hatch, following him after he ejected."

"How many chutes did you see after you egressed the falling plane?"

"I saw four chutes. I assumed they were the two pilots and maybe two of the three navigators."

They listened attentively to all my responses and eventually replied, "You are in a state of shock."

During my stay in the hospital, I was repeatedly asked how I got out or egressed. They asked each time, assuming I would respond differently. However, I gave the same answer whenever they asked me this question. Their response remained the same, too. "You are still in a state of shock, Lt. Mattocks."

Only I knew that I was neither excited nor in shock. Surprisingly, different officials came and asked the same question differently, but I gave each one the same answer.

One of them asked me, "Lt. Mattocks, how do you know that two of the four chutes you saw may have been the pilot's chute?"

"Because I saw the pilots eject. I even saw the aircraft commander look at me with sadness, as if he wanted to say sorry. He then ejected, and I immediately jumped to open the pilot's hatch but ended up going out of the aircraft command hatch." I explained to them.

The reality I told the officials intrigued them because they knew that if anyone had to perish in the plane, it would have to be me. And if there had to be two persons to perish, it would have been the instructor, navigator, and me. It would happen because we both had to jump out of the plane physically.

I was asked similar questions on and off until five or six o'clock in the morning. The dilemma that centered or resided in my statement was the reality of seeing me alive and in one piece, even after such a dangerous egress. The way I egressed the plane was completely wrong, different from the prescribed ways, and undoubtedly dangerous. It carried with it an assurance of death, yet I was standing there alive and reaching the Base even before everyone else.

As much as I knew about plane egress, I hadn't read about or seen anyone physically bailing out through the top hatch of a B-52 and living through it. I had never heard of such a thing happening before, not even after my incident. Therefore, it was hard for everyone to believe me and my statements as unmistakable.

Their disbelief in my statement turned into verified truth when Major Tulloch arrived back at the Base during the daybreak. He smiled with happiness and relief when he learned about my safe return. He felt content, thinking everyone on the flight had approached land safely. He had verified that I was still in the plane when he ejected and therefore had good reason to believe everyone had gotten out safely.

Major Tulloch's confirmation cleared up the investigating official's dilemma, but the investigation continued. They eventually believed that my answers weren't delivered in a state of shock. In the meantime, I peculiarly memorized all of the situations we went through, events, and circumstances regarding emergencies and the subsequent plane crash. I rehearsed assiduously to give accurate answers to the investigating officials.

Chapter 5

During the investigation process, I was made to answer numerous questions. I replied to every question attentively.

However, a few questions couldn't be answered. *"Why were you put through the same emergency in the B-52G simulator the day before?"* *"How did the simulator instructor know the precise date and time to set up the simulator with this specific emergency?"*

I was scheduled for training in the simulator to include normal and emergency procedures. It was the aircraft commander during this simulator flight.

On January 22, 1961, I was given clearance by the simulator instructor to take off in the simulator while he watched over me meticulously. After accomplishing the takeoff, I carried out normal procedures as commanded by the instructor. Afterward, the instructor began to put different types of emergencies in front of me to handle and make my way through them. I understood each and initiated precise procedures for corrective actions. Though emergencies were put forth, nothing unusual happened during the drill. Every emergency was tackled and overcome by corrective action. In the meantime, the instructor was writing my report in his logbook.

However, there arrived a twist in the end. At the end of the training flight, the simulator instructor initiated another emergency. This emergency was trickier as the instructor made a hole in the right main wing tank. For corrective action, I cut engines #5 and #6. I implemented appropriate actions to maintain proper electrical and hydraulic systems in this condition.

There was a potential control issue as the left wing became heavier than the right wing. Therefore, in order to assess the simulator's high characteristics just above landing speeches, I leveled off the slow movement of the hydraulic controls at 10,000 feet. I put down my flap as I slowed to a speed that was more than ten knots above landing speed.

After lowering the flap lever, the simulator quickly entered a slow right bank. We did everything I had tried in the simulator in "Keep One Niner," but just like the simulator, we spun out of control and simulated my ejection; we had to eject in this situation.

Only God's kindness and mercy could save a sinner like me and enable me to experience the fatal simulation that happened the following day, the outcome of which perplexed the elite, higher authorities, and those in high places because something that could not have allowed life to continue, despite being dangerous and hazardous, saved me.

As I watched helplessly and intently, I asked a question that my past simulator experience had led me to ponder. "As I had to climb the ladder from the top deck to the bottom deck, why didn't the aircraft commander warn us to bail out immediately?"

During the closing 30 seconds of the flight, he said, "Keep One Niner."

This was a serious and crucial question. However, at that moment, it didn't matter at all. There were little families that lost loved ones in the collision, so I am aware of the depth of their anguish. But I am also aware that God remained in charge. I was worried about how long it was going to take because I was the last one to physically bail out of the plane.

From a purely selfish point of view, I needed to bail out and egress the plane as soon as possible. As unbelievable as it sounds, I made the decision to detach my radio, seatbelt, and shoulder harness during the 30 seconds available to speed up my escape. But as soon as I reconnected my radio, everything stopped. I wouldn't have heard the order to bail out without the radio. I left my shoulder harness behind but rejoined my seatbelt. I reduced my escape time by turning 90 degrees right in my seat while keeping my left hand on the seatbelt lever.

When finally, the bailout command came, it didn't really matter. I could only take a single step towards the rear (opening to the lower deck) before being pinned to the floor due to the positional G-force caused by the spin to the right. While I was pinned to the floor of the airplane, my past life, including all the things that I had ever done, flashed in front of me. I thought about my present life and thought about things that I was into. Moreover, I dreamed of my future with my wife, my children, and my future children. My whole life flashed by, and it seemed like it passed faster than a day.

"Adam, there is no way you can escape," I said to myself.

At that unfortunate moment, I had nothing to do but accept death. I felt as if I would be the only one to die on this plane.

I was facing the rear when I was initially pinned to the floor and grayed out. When my sight began to return, I was facing forward and still pinned to the right side of the floor. I don't know how or when, nor by what means or manner, I was turned around. I was grateful to be in that specific location and position, although there was no possible way to escape. My plans—and actions—were to get to the lower deck so I could bail out.

The positive G-force was reduced, and my eyesight returned to normal.

The time it took for the plane to transition from one positive G to one negative G was roughly three seconds. I would only be able to leave during this time frame. At that time, many events were required to take place just before and throughout those three seconds. A hole or exit in the cockpit would have needed to be made by the aircraft commander blowing his hatch. He would have had to get out from under his hatch, both his seat and himself.

To escape from the commander's hatch on the left side of the aircraft, I would have needed to jump just in time for the airplane to spin at the proper speed. However, to travel from the inside to the outside, it was required that all of these events take place at the proper times and in the proper sequences.

Fortunately, the aforementioned events all took place at the proper times and in the proper sequence. The plane turned as I leaped straight forward down the right side, putting the hatch directly in front of me. I tried to pull myself through the hatch but was instead pulled or shoved through.

In the plane, only two people among the entire crew had to physically bail out: the navigator instructor and me. One had to bail out on the upper deck, while the other would bail out on the lower deck. However, it was advised later that both of us should bail out at the same hatch and on the lower deck. But the circumstances took a turn and caused me to escape or climb out of the top of the B-52.

Later, the investigation revealed that because I was trying to exit in the opposite direction from the other crew member when the jet entered negative "G," the negative G force helped me exit while impeding him from doing so. I was lifted out of the plane by the same G force that drew the other crew member back in. It was tragic to learn that the crew member on the flight had died.

I managed to escape the hatch with God's assistance, but I knew that the enormous vertical and horizontal stabilizers, moving at 180 knots, would smash my body into a greasy patch. Nevertheless, the spin that occurred while I was in the cockpit caused a twist in the fuselage between the bays for the two booms. I was in the cockpit when the tailpiece, which held the vertical and horizontal stabilizers, broke away and dropped from the fuselage.

Therefore, I knew that the danger that was waiting outside for me had been removed. I realized that my journey to the outside was fortunately and miraculously accomplished without harm and securely.

The glory and praise belong only to God.

However, by this time, my torments weren't over. The parachute functioned perfectly, but a moment before it was to fully blossom, the shock wave from the explosion collapsed it. It was a horrifying moment, and all I could say was, "Oh, God. Did you bring me out of that falling plane to go down in a streamer or tangled chute?"

Suddenly, the chute blossomed. It was indeed a miracle happening right in front of me. I immediately turned my focus toward the landing. As I looked at the ground, all I saw was fire—the kind that I hadn't witnessed till that day. It appeared as if someone had set the Earth on fire.

"Lord, I will land in the middle of the fire. And I don't see myself getting out alive from this deadly fire." I murmured to myself.

At this point, I had emotionally and spiritually accepted my death. I had less fear and more acceptance, which helped me relax my nerves in the parachute. Suddenly, I felt myself going away from the fire. The amazingly powerful wind blew me away from the fire and took me toward a cool forest packed with trees. It took me near a farmer's home that had just been plowed that same day.

I knew it was God and only God who could do such things. It's possible that some of them were coincidences and some weren't. The timing and sequence of the events were not random; rather, they were directed and controlled by a power superior to you and me. In addition, these cannot be attributed merely to luck because, in such a brief time, there isn't much luck to be had. Thus, the hands of the master were acting in our favor.

As mentioned earlier, my house was 70 miles away from Seymour Johnson Air Force Base. Specifically, my house was 62 miles southeast from Seymour Johnson Air Force Base, Goldboro , N.C., located in a small community called Belgrade, N.C., and at the time of the accident, in those days, my family didn't have a telephone. I knew that my wife must be wondering if I was alive after she heard of the crash flashing on the news. Therefore, once I was done giving answers to the investigating officials, I asked for permission to visit my home.

In response to my permission request, I was informed that since I wasn't in a stable state of mind, I couldn't drive. I requested that they contact the motorway patrol headquarters in Raleigh, North Carolina, to contact their highway patrolman in Maysville, N.C., in order to inform my wife of the crash and reassure her that I was okay.

After months passed following the "Keep One Niner" crash, things began to get back to normal. Flights began flowing regularly without incident. My personal life came back to normal, filled with joy and peace. In addition, with God's blessing to everything else, in July of the same year, my third child came into the world. My family expanded, and we then became a sweet family of parents and three children: one son and two daughters.

October 1961

I requested an annual leave to attend the homecoming game at North Carolina A&T University. As I hadn't attended the homecoming since my graduation, i.e., 1957, I had to be present for this one. At the time I made the request, I was assigned as a pilot on a flight with another B-52 crew, but since I had to go on annual leaves, I was replaced by a new pilot.

The game day arrived, and the weather in Greensboro, N.C., turned unpleasant with rain and thunderstorms. Therefore, I decided not to attend the homecoming and spent my annual leave doing something else. When I returned to duty on Monday, I saw a large crowd of wives and family members. They were sitting in the base operations area. As I checked in, I was informed that a plane that participated in the weekend "sky sheet" was missing.

Since the crew had reported their descent to level off at an extremely low level, no information was received from the plane. They leveled off at approximately 150 to 250 feet above the water altitude and over the Atlantic off the coast of New York to North Carolina. This was definitely a mission for the plane and its crew to demonstrate their abilities to fly under an enemy's radar system without being detected.

I personally knew the commander of that crew. He was a fine officer, an exceptional pilot, and a capable aircraft commander. He was indeed a great man. The moment I learned about the missing crew, I felt a different kind of grief and ache in my heart. I instantly became sad for the crew members and their family members, eagerly waiting for their loved ones to magically show up. It was then that I became attached to the families of the crew members and carried the guilt of them all, especially the officers, pilots, and copilots that flew the mission in my stead.

I didn't know what happened to the flight, but it got extremely challenging for me to stop the guilt self talk and my mind from thinking about the plane. I tried to imagine, analyze, or even understand whether my presence on the flight would have altered the outcome of this flight. Even to this day, I wonder in my mind, *if I were there in the plane, would I be able to see the danger before it took everything away with it?* I never got the answer, but my beliefs, in my God's mercy helps me remain positive.

Every morning, the families approached the Base expecting to receive good news about their loved ones. However, it wasn't just the families. I was there, too, reaching the Base regularly to listen to the good news. Sometimes, things did become excruciatingly problematic for me. I was swamped in a flood of guilt whenever I saw or encountered any family member, especially the officer who flew in as my replacement.

Time passed, and one day, the rescue teams found nothing to report. It was this information that faded our optimism. After another week of searching, the rescue personnel revealed that they couldn't find any proof that the plane had crashed. No planes or airplane pieces were discovered or observed. In addition, no crew members or even the personal belongings of crew members were discovered.

The rescue team's information puzzled my mind, and I found it hard to believe that an entire B-52 plane with its entire crew disappeared without any trace. It was incredibly unbelievable. Moreover, the plane was loaded with fuel and oil and had air in its tires; all such things had the capacity to float and spill oil on and in the water flow. Even the crew members had to wear their water gear when flying over a large body of water. In addition, all the seat cushions had the capacity to float.

What happened? Did this crew fly into the water by flying at the exact altitude or altimeter given? Or did the plane fly into the water due to pilot error? Or did an emergency occur at this low altitude? Or did the crew fly the plane someplace else? My tangled mind couldn't figure out what exactly happened on the damn flight!

Weeks passed, and the rescue team couldn't find any trace of the plane. On the other hand, the family members would regularly come to the base operation, waiting the entire time to hear some words of comfort. This went on for weeks until we received the words that confirmed our greatest nightmare, "The rescue is called off." The rescue team reported that there was little or no physical evidence available. Ultimately, the crew was declared missing, lost, or dead.

However, the declaration did not wrap up the situation in our minds. To us, there was no conclusion or end to the matter, as our hopes continued to linger.

As time passed, I went on with my life. However, every now and then, I would remember and be taunted in my mind with the same puzzling questions.

Apart from that, the situation at Seymour Johnson Air Force Base began to change. The crew members began to act or react based on their circumstances and thoughts. Most of the people at the Base knew that I should, by all reasonable standards, have been killed during the Keep One Niner flight. Also, the loss of the plane to which I was initially assigned as a pilot caused some problems within the squadron.

For example, when or if I were assigned to fly and the flight surgeon removed me for medical reasons, the crew who was scheduled to fly that particular plane would find something wrong with that plane or request another plane to fly.

After a few such incidents, I received orders to Loring AFB, Maine, as an instructor pilot in the B-52G simulator.

In 1962, when I arrived at Loring AFB, Maine, I maintained my professional flying with the Boomer wing and flew with combat crews on a training mission and a combat 24-hour' mission. I spent most of my time training pilots in the simulator. We had a stationed simulator for the pilots at Loring AFB. We also had a mobile simulator to service Griffith AFB, New York, Seymour Johnson AFB, and Warner Robin AFB, GA.

During one of my visits to Seymour Johnson to teach pilots in the simulators, I had the chance to instruct the pilot who attempted to give me an unsatisfactory performance rating. I preprogrammed the simulator for several emergencies. The pilot took off with his copilot, and they ascended to the designated altitude. All of the anticipated emergencies were covered. Before departure, twice throughout the flight, and once before the landing drop, I set the pressure. I increased the altimeter's setting to 10,000 feet as part of the emergency and inspections and gave them permission to descend for landing after the mission. They followed all the customary steps. Later, I told them to descend to 2,500 feet and report back from there. Unfortunately, the simulator collapsed, and all the lights went out when they arrived at 10,000. I explained that they had crashed when he asked what was wrong. I restarted the simulator and re-lit the room. I commanded them to examine the altimeter setting because, at that point, both altimeters were still 10,000 feet off.

I discussed with them how dangerous it was to fly the crew and aircraft along their path at an altitude that was 10,000 feet lower than what they were actually instructed. I explained to them that this simulator crashed because it was 10,000 below what the altimeter indicated.

Notwithstanding the seriousness of the pilot's error, I did not rate him as unreliable or unsatisfactory. Everything this pilot attempted to make me give an unsatisfactory rating was unsuccessful. Even with justification, I did not assign him an unsatisfactory rating since I believed he would no longer make the same pilot error based on his demeanor.

I continued to train the pilots at Seymour Johnson AFB and other AFBs.

To keep up my expertise and skills as a combat-ready pilot, I continued to fly the B-52G. I once took off on a flight in the fall of 1963 and completed a second 24-hour trip that included parts of Canada and Greenland.

This was a 24-hour combat-ready mission. As we got closer to Canadian airspace, we asked for permission to enter and pass through its airspace. The Canadian Airspace carried out an extraordinary and noteworthy number of tests to ensure our identity as being friendly and establish whether we were friends or foes. Our response to their previous challenge was followed by the words "*20 seconds before Bing Bang.*"

It broadcast over the command radio, which meant we had been attacked by an atomic warhead. We all took a deep, disconcerting sigh, and a creepy silence took over the entire plane.

Immediately following the "Big Bang" statement coming over the command radio, there was another command voice that stated, "Disregard, Disregard, over."

We all took a deep breath as the aircraft commander responded, "Roger."

Subsequently, we entered Canadian airspace and kept flying through it on our way to Loring AFB. But, as we contemplated what had just occurred, the remaining time on the flight was filled with wonder and awe.

After we returned to Loring AFB, we entered the traffic pattern. Later, we landed and taxied toward the parking ramp. As we were about to exit the plane, somebody informed us that we couldn't leave the plane. They told us to be seated in our respective positions while the plane was refueled and serviced.

The entire monitoring of the plane was carried out. All systems were checked and re-serviced. This, however, wasn't a normal procedure. But we didn't interfere and let them carry out the examination.

However, while we landed and taxied our plane in the parking ramp, I noticed that planes were lined up for five minutes, and one plane would take off every minute. We thought of the situation as a practice alert, but the presence of an unusual number of security guards was bewildering. The security guards were present almost in every area with their dogs, and it seemed that each guard and his dog were protecting one B-52G.

Until our plane was refueled, we remained restricted inside our plane, and none of them talked to us. Subsequently, we began conversing with each other, sharing the unusual practices we had all been noticing since our landing. We talked to determine if all of us were thinking about the same thing or if the base was in a real state of emergency. At that time, I knew that the US was in the midst of the Cold War with the USSR. However, by that time, we weren't informed of any heightened tension between the two rivals.

All of us conversed for approximately one hour, pondering all the possible reasons our minds could think of. Soon thereafter, another crew was sent to replace us. We couldn't understand the reason behind everything, as we had just completed a "24-hour airborne alert mission" and had spent another hour confined in the plane. Since the replacement crew was coming, we exited the plane and were escorted directly to the debriefing room. On the way, we saw the replacement crew but didn't manage to have a word with them.

We entered the briefing room and asked to be seated.

The head investigating officer stated, "I understand that you must be wondering what's going on."

We looked at him with bewilderment but joy at finally getting the answers. He informed us that President Kennedy had blockaded Cuba. Considering the condition of Cuba, the US Air Force was stopping and searching for any Russian ships or missiles being deployed in Cuba. We debriefed our mission to the officer and, later, got a brief for our other mission and target study.

The blockade of Cuba had heightened the tension in the USA, and the US forces and combat crews were on high alert throughout the world. An all-out war situation had erupted; however, contrary to what everyone thought, the tension didn't escalate into a full-fledged war. Soon, the crisis was terminated, and it restored mobility throughout the USA and the world.

Similarly, military life returned to normal, and surprisingly, the officer who gave me an unsatisfactory rating at Seymour Johnson AFB gave me a satisfactory rating later. A satisfactory rating did not have to be justified by the rater, nor could the person being rated adequately invalidate a satisfactory rating. I knew that any performance rating below 'excellent' would hinder the officer from getting a promotion. I could say that considering the reductions and cutbacks during 1962, 1963, and 1964.

The intentions of my rater in giving me a low rating were to get me kicked off the flying status. Unfortunately, his unjustified rating affected my career, and my promotion opportunities got declined due to the Air Force's 20/10 reduction in the force program. Introduced in the 1960s, this program entailed that officers with ratings less than excellent would be automatically passed over.

Unfortunately, I only learned about it after I received a satisfactory rating, which couldn't be challenged or changed by anyone.

I went through every possible level of headquarters in Washington, D.C., to try to get the rating changed because I knew they weren't giving it to me based on my performance. However, during the appeal process, I was informed that the rater's opinion of the junior officers with a satisfactory or higher rating but less than excellent would not be changed by anyone in the system, regardless of the truth or facts behind it.

Regardless of what I did to get the ratings changed, they were never changed and remained in my records forever. It harmed my career and destroyed me. I lost a piece of my heart when I suffered the cruel injustice that happened to me. For them, I was a black man who achieved more than they thought he could. The rater couldn't see a black man achieving success; therefore, he played a malicious game on me. However, the rating was officially meant for the bad, who could challenge God's plans. He flipped the case and took what was best for me from it. I still have that Cadillac in my room, just as a reminder of that scenario, and ever since, I have owned nine Cadillacs. All thanks to my God, who has always blessed me.

Chapter 6

Finally, the time to get out of the service arrived.

As I headed out of the service and to new beginnings, I sensed the fierce competition in the airline career field. I placed my application for Tran World Airlines, United Airlines, National Airlines, and Eastern Airlines. Later, I realized that other Air Force pilots, who were caught in the 20/10 program, like me, had applied to these airlines as well.

The qualifications required to get enrolled as a pilot with any one of these airlines were minimal. They required a qualification of high school education, 400 hours of flying time in any aircraft, and an FAA license. On the other hand, in 1964, when I applied for these jobs, I had a college education, approximately 1400 hours of flying time, a commercial license, a multi-engine land, and an instrument rating that authorized me to fly in all types of weather.

Based on my credentials and my mind-blowing record, each one of the airlines showed interest in hiring me. However, every one of them said they could only consider me after my separation from the service. Therefore, I inquired about the procedure and got authorization to conclude my services in 1964.

Subsequently, Tran World Airline set up an interview in the early spring of 1964. When I arrived there, I saw eighteen other applicants waiting for the interview. Surprisingly, all of them were white males. Later, I realized that, according to my number of flying hours and the conversation circulating among the other applicants, I was the fourth highest qualified candidate.

After waiting for a while, I was finally called for an interview. During the interview, I was asked only two questions: first, if my social security number was correct, and second, if my home address was accurate. The interview concluded, and when the results came out, TWA hired the three applicants above me and cut them out of the process. The next person would have been me.

Approximately three or four weeks later, I received a letter from them stating that I was indeed qualified for the post, but unfortunately, they had selected someone better qualified. In reality, all nineteen applicants were very qualified. The fifteen white male applicants below me were denied selection based on racially discriminatory practices and policies readily used during the 1960s.

Unfortunately, I had a similar heartbreaking experience with three other airlines. Even the wording stated in every airline's denial letter was the same. The paragraphs were identical as if the same legal officer had prepared the letters. The only difference I could see was the name of the airline. I felt awful when, even after having such a brilliant record, I couldn't gain employment as a pilot in any airline.

At that time, there wasn't a term like 'glass ceiling theory,' but it was readily practiced everywhere, albeit without recognition. Certain job fields were completely closed to blacks, and the probability of their opening for a man of color was thin—in fact, negligible. However, I stayed away from despair and relied on God because I knew that only he had control over everything.

When I left military service in June 1964, I returned to my hometown of Jacksonville, N.C., and the small community of Belgrade, N.C. While I was seeking employment through the North Carolina Employment Service, I worked with my father, Mr. Ira W. Mattocks Sr., in the meantime. My father had previously trained four of his six sons as brick and block masons and carpenters in the building trades. He owned a business as a subcontractor. I invested a lot of time working and learning with him.

In addition, I got actively involved in the local community and civil rights activities, similar to my college days in 1953–1957. I actively encouraged and raised my voice for human and civil rights at the University of North Carolina and at A&T in Greensboro, North Carolina.

We started integrating the movie theater while I was still working at A&T. According to the managers and staff, black students had to watch the movies upstairs, while white students had to view them below. These A&T students who physically waited were white. There were a few white students attending A&T, though we were unaware of this at the time. The student's plan was to replace the black actors in the film who had blond hair, blue or grey eyes, and other physical traits associated with the Caucasian race and could not be recognized as black by appearance with an actor who had black-looking physical traits.

On Saturday afternoons, the couples would position themselves so that they would arrive at the ticket booth right after the manager attempted to separate them by sending the dark-skinned black student upstairs and the light-skinned student downstairs. Some, however, would not be divided, and the management would either send both upstairs or downstairs or turn both away. This plan of action persisted for a few weeks. After some delay and a potentially hazardous confrontation, the sign that read "colored persons upstairs" was finally taken down, and the movie theater was integrated. Every Saturday, we would get together and laugh about everything that happened, including the experiences of each couple.

Males and females who agreed to be separated and were assigned to the downstairs area would try to sit close to one another or occasionally form groups. One of the groups of men with light skin would make an effort to ascend the stairs to meet his purported girlfriend in order to harass the manager or the female working the ticket counter. However, a man and woman with very light skin who went upstairs occasionally went downstairs once or twice after returning upstairs to perplex and annoy the theater managers who were on duty and were by this point so perplexed that they didn't know who had been sent upstairs or downstairs or why white people wanted to sit upstairs. The theater was desegregated without incident or an arrest by the authorities. The plan was to portray a problem that would be difficult but solvable, with opportunities and realistic solutions for all parties.

I had finished my military service and was now back in my hometown. I actively participated in the civil rights movement as a lifelong member of the National Association for the Advancement of Colored People (NAACP), and I was chosen to head the branch's executive committee. I also collaborated with residents on a grass-roots level to execute the Economic Opportunity Act (EOA), which offered some assistance to underprivileged families in the county.

The community-based organizations chose a representative from each organization to sit on an action committee that would conduct research, plan, establish, and, if necessary, operate an organization that required those who required the services outlined in the EOA to be involved in the planning, support, and delivery of service and assistance through the use of volunteers, advisors, and recipients of goods and services. I was chosen to lead the committee's action. The committee had put a lot of effort into completing several surveys, including surveys of community needs, present service delivery, population, income percentage, housing, employment by race, level of education by race, and many more. This committee carried out an analysis and created numerous profiles.

In the meantime, the organization was built, and the bylaws and constitution were developed by the committee. The committee recommended the chartered name of EDUCO, and all the actions and documents were approved by all the participating groups. Afterward, the documents were forwarded to the state office for chartering, recognition, and establishment as a non-profit corporation in the state of North Carolina.

After going through and completing the filing process , EDUCO was granted a charter to get involved in any activities provided by the Economic Opportunity Association (EOA). The action committee, after that, initiated planning and developing programs and services to meet the needs and reduce the problems identified through surveys. Several programs were developed, approved, and submitted to Washington, DC, to the Headquarters Economic Opportunity Office. Fortunately, numerous projects got approved; among them were the Head Start and the neighborhood Youth Corps programs.

In the Washington, D.C., office, we met Sergeant Shriver several times. Our first meeting took place, followed by the approval notification of Head Start and the neighborhood Youth Corps programs. However, before EDUCO could receive the funding, the local county commission would have to designate EDUCO as the agency in Onslow County, N.C., authorized to administer the approved funds at the local level. There was another requirement that stated the agency designated by the county commissions must have a board of directors made up of "one-third members of the group to be serviced, one-third public elected officials or their representatives, and one-third local businesses and agency personnel in the area service."

At this point, we realized we had a serious problem to manage.

EDUCO and all the volunteers working in it were black. Moreover, other agencies working in the state and county had reported that there wasn't any family or individual left in the area whose requirements needed to be met yet. However, the reality was quite the opposite. There were still some families who were still living underprivileged lives and their problems were still unresolved. This was all highlighted by our surveys. Some families were neither aware of nor in a position to seek out services that they were eligible for that were available, while other necessary services were not available. As many black people have throughout the years, we were forced to consider the possibility that, even if our efforts fell well short of our aspirations and dreams, they would nevertheless have been worthwhile.

Our approach was initiated with our first strategy, which entailed seeking out agency heads that we felt would have the least problems working with black people. We looked for agencies that were willing to work as equal partners on the board with the desire to assist the deprived families while keeping racial and family differences aside. Since our board of directors would consist of nine directors, we decided to look for three to serve on the board.

However, we were able to find only one agency in the area. She was the local head of the local health department.

At the same time, we met the county commission. We had a discussion about the letter and our meeting with Mr. Shriver. We presented a copy of EDUCO's charter, bylaws, and constitution to the commission for review. The commission declared the documents valid after reviewing them but wanted their attorney to keep a copy of all the information for further study. They informed us that they would get back to us.

A month passed, after which the attorney told me he wasn't done reviewing our documents when we met at one of the commissioner's sessions. As the start of school drew near, we decided that the board of education could sponsor the two programs until our board of directors was fully compliant and the county commissioners had named EDUCO, Inc. as the community action agency. This was done out of concern for the children and a desire to ensure that they received the services and help that were available to them. After several months of stalling, the county commissioners eventually convened in private.

They gave us a new charter for a non-profit organization and named it Onslow County Fund, Inc. The charter, bylaws, and constitution were almost exact replicas of those of EDUCO, Inc. We thought the commissioners gave them permission to create their own documents using language taken from ours. This encounter sparked the conflict that would grow over the following months. There were now two groups that could help underprivileged and needy students, families, and children. But neither of the boards of directors complied with the demands. On the surface, the Onslow County Fund, Inc. board of directors seemed to satisfy the standards.

They had the designations and the appointees by the commissioners, and they had one-third of agency heads in their hands. This included the one from the Health Department that was initially EDUCO, Inc. We learned, the only agency head we found earlier in our area resigned too from the board of EDUCO, Inc. and was forced to join the board of the Onslow County Fund, Inc. out of protest. The board of education appointed black educators, including a black principal and black teachers, who were not members of the underprivileged population or group and were not chosen by the underprivileged group to serve as their representatives.

The board of directors of EDUCO, Inc. put out a merger proposal for Onslow County Fund, Inc (OCF). and EDUCO, Inc. during the following few months. After the merger was successfully accomplished, the two boards worked smoothly with each other for a few months. They felt secure, and their projects got successful. In order to prevent the commission and a few specific agency officials from dissolving or undoing the members of the two boards' sincere efforts, OCF, Inc. would submit the compromise to them.

I was aware that it was only a matter of time before the person or people in charge of OCF, Inc. came up with the notion to select a welfare beneficiary for their board of directors under the pretense that they were speaking on behalf of and for the disadvantaged group. Nonetheless, EDUCO, Inc. made sure that the minutes of the open meeting where the representatives were elected in each region were recorded. Even though this was obvious, well-known, and supported, the rule that one group that may be disadvantaged may not prevent another disadvantaged from receiving necessary services and or help still applies.

My committee met with Mr. Shriver once more to discuss our goal to support and help low-income and disadvantaged families and family members. We had frank and real conversations with the staff at the meeting. Various alternatives, opportunities, and strategies were put forth and suggested.

The opportunity for the merger was out, and we still had plenty of low-income and disadvantaged individuals on our team as well as some businesspeople working with us. Therefore, Washington agreed to demand that OCF, Inc. offer a specific board of directors. As a result of this choice, I joined the group of EDUCO board members who afterward joined the board of directors for OCF, Inc.

Onslow County Fund, Inc.'s board of directors was diversified, and they now met all the requirements of the law. After this, the new board started to seek a development grant. The staff required a development grant to plan programs and services for the low-income population. We developed four positions, i.e., Director, Assistant Director, Bookkeeper, and Secretary, for the smooth implementation of the development grant.

While some EDUCO members got elated with the news because they had worked so hard to acquire their deserved recognition and grants, they were happy because they now didn't have to share their funded programs with any organization called "OCF." Because the joint board, with two-thirds of its members from OCF, would not consider any black people who served on the action committee for EDUCO and wrote the initial programs that were funded, the board would then recommend one of the employees for the Assistant Director position.

Finally, the procedure was settled, and the interviewing session was initiated.

The action committee wanted someone from their group to be considered for the position of Assistant Director because black people couldn't be considered for any directorial-level positions. We soon came to see how terrible and pervasive racism was in this eastern North Carolina County as we continued. We also came to understand the extent of the black community's anger at the majority's bad faith and unfair treatment of them. But more disappointing than that was that the black people were now split up among themselves. While some of them rallied around the appalling situations and predicaments many white and black families were in, others did so because of how white people had continued to treat black people.

I understood that we had a challenging task as we worked to promote racial harmony among black people and inform the white majority of the detrimental effects of racism on all races. We struggled with the learned behavior and beliefs of the white people, who strongly believed that no black person was or would be capable of managing money or administering programs that would significantly impact or improve the conditions of many white families.

A black male who was involved in the action committee and unemployed at the time was advised by a few other black people and me to apply for the assistant director position. He applied for the director post instead of the assistant director position since he didn't want to be the assistant director. I had personally analyzed the staffing pattern and concluded that there was only one position that the white person felt a black person could be placed in—it was the assistant director position. They believed the director might use this position to their advantage, turning it into a mere figurehead without any assignments or responsibilities. Moreover, the pay was extremely low, only a few dollars above that of the clerical staff.

I was aware that whites wouldn't appoint a black secretary to deal with the white directors and agency communications since doing so would give that person a chance to learn too much about the agency's operations and hiring procedures. For the same reasons they wouldn't hire a black secretary, I also knew the white members wouldn't hire a black bookkeeper because I was not aware of any black people working in the aforementioned types of positions in any state or local organizations in this area in 1965.

Even though the assistant director position paid significantly less than what I was making as a brick mason in my father's building company before April 1966 or 1965, I still applied for it. I understood that the wages would be adjusted accordingly once the company was completely formed. After I split rank and placed an application, some of my comrades opposed and objected to my being considered for selection.

When the interviews began, I told the board that I, along with the NAACP branch in Onslow County, would support the idea that the candidates chosen for each post should have the greatest qualifications possible and that we would challenge the decision using every legal strategy if the most competent candidates in each job field had not been chosen.

"The information you have concerning the NAACP opposing my

selection is erroneous. I am the president of the Onslow County branch of NAACP, and the NAACP supports this effort of a fair and objective process." This was the response that we received in return, however.

Chapter 7

In April 1966, I was appointed as the Assistant Director for Onslow County Fund, Inc (OCF, Inc). My job responsibilities included writing programs, making personal policies, designing operations and grievance procedures, staffing, and preparing budget requirements.

The staffing recommendations submitted to the board included an executive director, deputy director, secretary, bookkeeper, assistant bookkeeper, head start director, assistant head start director, teacher, and other staff personnel. It also included the neighborhood youth corps director and multi-purpose center director.

Later, the board further divided the deputy director position into two assistant director positions. It divided the deputy's salary between two people. The plan was approved and sent to the regional office in Washington, D.C. The regional office approved the rest of the plan except for having two assistant director positions. It recommended the title be changed to Deputy Director.

Therefore, I was tasked with amending the personnel staffing policy to conform to the approved staffing plan by the regional office. I could see that it would be challenging to get the Deputy Director's salary where it should be and accurately describe the duties and responsibilities. It was a challenge that I had to deal with, and it brought positive results.

So, I began working on it.

I accurately designated all duties in the position description setting. I added the salary between the Executive Director and Project Director's salaries. When the plan was set forth for approval, the salary scale got approved, and the deputy's salary was brought into line with the duties and responsibilities of the position.

The director and I had a good relationship, as he was one of my teachers during my high school days. He was hired straight out of the school system. Therefore, I asked him to send me all the correspondence once he was done reading it. I wanted to know the material regulations and requirements to ensure our organization was in compliance.

When the Executive Director resigned, I was promoted temporarily to the position of Executive Director. While serving in this position on a temporary basis, I submitted an application for the position. Fortunately, every person on my staff, whether black, white, male, or female, signed a petition requesting that the board and its personnel committee permanently select me as the Executive Director.

Subsequently, I was promoted to the Executive Director position.

Both the organization and the number of volunteers from the public, business, and nonprofit sectors increased. The services offered by Head Start, Neighborhood Youth Corps, literacy, and self-help programs and activities helped children of all ages develop while strengthening and reinforcing families, communities, and even entire counties.

The Community Act Program (CAP) in Duplin County merged with those run by OFT, Inc., in 1974. Onslow County Fund, Inc.'s name was changed to Onslow/Duplin Counties Community Action Agency due to the expanded service area. Later, the name was modified to Onslow, Duplin, and Pender Community Action Agency. Before the name of the program was amended to include any county within "Region P" of the state of North Carolina, additional counties requested these organizations to manage the community action program. The contemporary name as of this writing is "Region "P" Community Action Agency.

The agency not only enhanced the families' lives but brought a wider understanding of equal economic and employment opportunities. There were two acts that were responsibly exercised by our organization, i.e., the Equal Employment Opportunity Act and the Equal Economic Opportunity Act. Moreover, we encouraged employee diversity in the workplace in order to have representatives from every population who needed to be served. Likewise, the banking institutions where we deposited our funds were directed to employ persons with the characteristics of the community served. We made considerable progress in most of the areas and even recruited qualified applicants for job openings.

In 1974, I resigned from the organization for better employment.

I actively worked with the NACCP during my tenure in the organization,. The branch was actively carrying out the recruitment of blacks who were between 25% and 40% employed, with a national average unemployment rate of less than 5%. In addition to that, the organization placed greater emphasis on the desegregated system of students and teachers in the classrooms.

As the NAACP recruited and worked with potential employees, we heard over and over again the same words, "He (or she) is overqualified."

It was difficult to comprehend how black applicants were divided into two groups by white companies. These were that they "were overqualified for everything" or "were not qualified for anything at all." However, we were aware that some of the candidates we recommended possessed extra expertise, knowledge, and skills in addition to those needed for the particular position.

Although these individuals would have been valuable assets to the company if another employer were to hire them in the near future, who knows? They might end up becoming your spokesperson for your products or services. Employers today and in the past have lost valuable workers who may have improved their companies' operations.

We actively took part in the desegregation of our public school system. We drafted a plan and hoped to carry out the integration process in a smooth manner. From 1954 to 1958, there were three black elementary schools in Onslow County: Belgrade Elementary School, Richland's Elementary School,, Silverdale Elementary School, and Georgetown Elementary School. However, there was only one high school called Georgetown High School that encompassed grades 9 to 12. It accommodated black students from across the county.

In addition to that, transportation was initially a problem in rural areas. Originally, only white students were transported by bus, leaving blacks with no option other than walking or having their parents take them to school. Later, the system was changed, and blacks were transported to school in separate school buses. It was gruesome that travelers going through the same roads and having the same destination were being transported in separate buses. This practice continued for years until we raised our voices. Then, the issue of segregated buses came to the forefront as a hot topic.

Separate but equal had never worked as it was intended to.

For instance, none of the white schools within the county could compete, nor were they equal with Jacksonville High School. Although Georgetown High School was accredited in 1957 and was the only school in the county to be accredited, it could not compete with the new Jacksonville High School during the late sixties.

Some black students sought admission to schools that had previously only accepted white students due to the desegregation criteria and freedom of choice laws. However, I couldn't find any white students who had applied to attend a school that was formerly all-black. The percentage of black enrollment did not achieve the proponent's desired results. However, it met and exceeded the opponent's desired results.

If a school system relies primarily on freedom of choice to accomplish integration, enrollment must increase dramatically compared to the time when freedom of choice was unsuccessful. The school board was sued by the NAACP North Carolina Conference, the local NAACP branch, and the NAACP Legal Defense Fund. The local branch kept monitoring the school board's progress.

The school board, therefore, was forced to implement further desegregation strategies as a result. In addition, "grade leveling" was used, in which all students in grades '1 through 6' and '7 through 9' who resided in certain school attendance zones, respectively, were leveled. In addition, there was another way called school zoning. The concept of "school zoning" stipulates that all high school students who reside in a specific high school zone must attend that high school.

The practice of "closing schools" was another one. The county's sole black high school was being looked at for closure. For all black kids in the county who graduated from high school or were enrolled there, "Georgetown High" served as the model. The closure of this high school aroused a lot of curiosity and worries in the black community. To maintain Georgetown High as one of the top high schools, the black community battled.

Moreover, our hopes dwindled when we learned that the county school board had decided to implement the school zoning method, which required all black students in the four outlined townships to attend the four previously all-white schools. It took away approximately 75% of Georgetown's high school students and left approximately 25% of them.

In Jacksonville Township, the old Jacksonville High School was designated as a junior high and made into the new Jacksonville High School and Georgetown High School. Consequently, the black community fought to keep Georgetown High School as one of the two high schools in Jacksonville Township. We requested to keep both schools in their respective zones, and students belonging to either zone would attend the respective high school.

Sadly, the black community's request was viewed as a dilemma, something that couldn't be accepted. The new integrated high school performed below par with the new Jacksonville high school and needed urgent improvement. The black community put forth another suggestion, even though there was a difference of opinion within the black community too. The black community requested to make the junior high like the old Jacksonville High School.

At that moment, when the black community put forth this idea, someone burned down part of the Georgetown facility and the gym. The fire caused such severe destruction that most of the high school's structures became unusable and remained unviable for the students. But the elementary school located on the same campus didn't sustain significant damage.

As the county grew, the recommendation to include technical institutes in Jacksonville and the Onslow County area was considered. The idea was presented to enhance the education and training opportunities in the respective townships. Yet again, the black community activated their efforts and suggested that the remaining classrooms and elementary schools should be established as technical institutes. Fortunately, our efforts were successful.

During the period of school integration or desegregation, the black community got split. Blacks didn't get split because of the objectives and goals of integration, but the methods planned or used to achieve the goals were different than what they had anticipated. The difference in methodology caused the community to drift in two different directions, with one group holding to one plan while the other went another way.

We knew that if Georgetown High School remained segregated, it would never be able to obtain the resources it needed to become competitive with Jacksonville High School. At that time, all of the school board members and commissioners were white males, and the majority of them were from Jacksonville Township, with their white children going to Jacksonville Senior High.

According to the experience of black schools in this area and specifically, according to my experience, if a teacher received a textbook at all or kids received a textbook to use, they were two to three years old when we got it. As a result, even if you scored an "A" on a test based on information from the old books, you might only score a "C" or "B" on a test based on the updated information in the new books.

This automatically placed black students at a disadvantage academically, which was not the fault of the students themselves but rather a systematic or systemic issue. Beginning in the segregated elementary school, this negative systemic effect persisted through the black high school and black college.

It became apparent, as previously indicated, when I met with my fellow 2nd Lieutenants in the USAF from the Air Force Academy and other Ivy League colleges after graduating from my black institution. This disadvantage, which refers to a lack of specific knowledge or practical expertise, was discovered during the initial test and evaluation at Lackland AFB. However, by completing the brief training there, I was able to acquire the essential knowledge or expertise because it was both accessible and available. As a result, I graduated among the top few students who were given the task of going to flight school in order to become an AF pilot.

This negative approach to the system affected every black student during the "separate but equal" school system.

The technical institute was located in the Georgetown facility and stayed there until its requirements caused it to relocate to its current location. Currently, it is located on Western Boulevard in Jacksonville and offers its services as a community college.

During the fifties and sixties in Eastern North Carolina, jobs and job assignments were totally determined by the race and sex of the applicants. All technical, managerial, supervisory, and leadership positions in the 105 skilled and semi-skilled job categories were considered or designated for white males. Non-technical and non-managerial, secretarial, clerical, and such jobs were designated for white females. The heavy labor jobs and few semi-skill jobs were for black males, and the light labor and maid-type jobs and such jobs were for black women. Whites, especially white men, had identified a standard of hiring for blacks that they should not rise above. These standards included dilapidated housing, old, worn-out cars, second-hand clothing, etc.

Jobs and work assignments in Eastern North Carolina throughout the 1950s and 1960s were solely based on the applicants' racial and sexual identities. In the skilled and semi-skilled employment categories, all technical, management, supervisory, and leadership jobs were prioritized or earmarked for white men. In addition, white women were only allowed to work in non-managerial, secretarial, and clerical positions.

For black men, there were few semi-skilled employment opportunities and heavy labor positions; for black women, there were maid positions and light labor positions. White people, and white men in particular, had established a threshold for hiring black people that they should not surpass. These requirements included worn-out vehicles, worn-out homes, used clothing, etc.

Even though many black people were undoubtedly talented in the agricultural and construction industries since their ancestors used slave labor to create homes, fancy buildings, plantations, and other types of structures for their slave owners, when these black men applied for this paid employment, the heirs of the slave owner judged them unqualified and inept due to their personal agendas or their prejudice. They were required to take the tasks that were offered, and frequently this involved training the young white supervisor and other whites placed in positions of authority, as well as completing some supervisory functions without being paid.

The local NAACP chapter and the black community started looking for jobs, and we began tracking down competent black job candidates. We provided the white companies and business community with a list of highly qualified black candidates for their posted opportunities in response to their claims that they could not locate blacks who were qualified for their employment. As expected, two categories of excuses started to come our way. The applicant was overqualified, according to one justification, and the position was already occupied, according to another.

Thank God that white people who cooperated with us throughout the Civil Rights Movement were sent in as applicants right away. The manager would examine these candidates and, in some circumstances, give them the same positions that the black applicants were told the position had been filled.

www.ingramcontent.com/pod-product-compliance
Lightning Source LLC
Chambersburg PA
CBHW020920140626
46545CB00015B/1024